D1520471

GLOBALVIEWPOINTS

Juvenile Crime

Other Books of Related Interest:

At Issue Series
Guns and Crime

Should the Legal Drinking Age Be Lowered?

Current Controveries Series
Family Violence

Introducing Issues with Opposing Viewpoints Series
Gangs

Gun Control

Issues That Concern You Series
Gun Violence

Risky Teen Behavior

Opposing Viewpoints Series
Juvenile Crime

Teens at Risk

GLOBALVIEWPOINTS

Juvenile Crime

Margaret Haerens, Book Editor

GREENHAVEN PRESS
A part of Gale, Cengage Learning

GALE
CENGAGE Learning·

Detroit • New York • San Francisco • New Haven, Conn • Waterville, Maine • London

Elizabeth Des Chenes, *Director, Publishing Solutions*

© 2013 Greenhaven Press, a part of Gale, Cengage Learning

Gale and Greenhaven Press are registered trademarks used herein under license.

For more information, contact:
Greenhaven Press
27500 Drake Rd.
Farmington Hills, MI 48331-3535
Or you can visit our Internet site at gale.cengage.com

For product information and technology assistance, contact us at

Gale Customer Support, 1-800-877-4253
For permission to use material from this text or product, submit all requests online at www.cengage.com/permissions

Further permissions questions can be emailed to permissionrequest@cengage.com

Articles in Greenhaven Press anthologies are often edited for length to meet page requirements. In addition, original titles of these works are changed to clearly present the main thesis and to explicitly indicate the author's opinion. Every effort is made to ensure that Greenhaven Press accurately reflects the original intent of the authors. Every effort has been made to trace the owners of copyrighted material.

Cover image copyright © Caro/Alamy.

LIBRARY OF CONGRESS CATALOGING-IN-PUBLICATION DATA

Juvenile crime / Margaret Haerens, book editor.
   p. cm. -- (Global viewpoints)
  Includes bibliographical references and index.
  ISBN 978-0-7377-6267-9 (hbk.) -- ISBN 978-0-7377-6443-7 (pbk.)
 1. Juvenile delinquency. I. Haerens, Margaret.
  HV9069.J7782 2012
  364.36--dc23
                                      2012025358

Printed in Mexico
1 2 3 4 5 6 7 16 15 14 13 12

Contents

Chapter 1: Trends in Juvenile Crime and Punishment

In some countries of Central America, youth gang violence is considered to be a serious national security threat. In response, El Salvador employs a more repressive approach; Costa Rica utilizes repressive tactics, but also preventative and rehabilitative policies; and Nicaragua focuses on a more liberal approach of prevention, rehabilitation, and a balanced perspective on the problem of youth crime.

Chapter 2: Risk Factors for Juvenile Crime

Although the election of the Scottish National Party (SNP) has marked a return to a less authoritarian approach to juvenile crime in the country, there are still reforms that could be made to better address the risk factors of juvenile crime. Two key reforms are raising the age of criminal responsibility in Scotland and finding alternatives to reformatories.

Chapter 3: Debates over the Juvenile Justice System

Chapter 4: Juvenile Justice System Reforms

Since the ratification of the United Nations Convention on the Rights of the Child, there has been significant progress in establishing a fair and effective juvenile justice system in a number of eastern European and central Asian countries. The treatment of juvenile offenders in Albania, Azerbaijan, Kazakhstan, Turkey, and the Ukraine can still be improved, however.

Ukraine is developing a new approach to juvenile crime, one that ensures the protection of children's rights and corresponds to international standards of juvenile justice. Improvements include better cooperation between service agencies; clearly defined roles for officials in the system; and the close involvement of communities and civil society institutions in the social reintegration of young offenders.

Foreword

> "*The problems of all of humanity can only be solved by all of humanity.*"
> —*Swiss author Friedrich Dürrenmatt*

Global interdependence has become an undeniable reality. Mass media and technology have increased worldwide access to information and created a society of global citizens. Understanding and navigating this global community is a challenge, requiring a high degree of information literacy and a new level of learning sophistication.

Building on the success of its flagship series, Opposing Viewpoints, Greenhaven Press has created the Global Viewpoints series to examine a broad range of current, often controversial topics of worldwide importance from a variety of international perspectives. Providing students and other readers with the information they need to explore global connections and think critically about worldwide implications, each Global Viewpoints volume offers a panoramic view of a topic of widespread significance.

Drugs, famine, immigration—a broad, international treatment is essential to do justice to social, environmental, health, and political issues such as these. Junior high, high school, and early college students, as well as general readers, can all use Global Viewpoints anthologies to discern the complexities relating to each issue. Readers will be able to examine unique national perspectives while, at the same time, appreciating the interconnectedness that global priorities bring to all nations and cultures.

Material in each volume is selected from a diverse range of sources, including journals, magazines, newspapers, nonfiction books, speeches, government documents, pamphlets, organization newsletters, and position papers. Global Viewpoints is truly global, with material drawn primarily from international sources available in English and secondarily from US sources with extensive international coverage.

Features of each volume in the Global Viewpoints series include:

- An **annotated table of contents** that provides a brief summary of each essay in the volume, including the name of the country or area covered in the essay.

- An **introduction** specific to the volume topic.

- A **world map** to help readers locate the countries or areas covered in the essays.

- For each viewpoint, an **introduction** that contains notes about the author and source of the viewpoint explains why material from the specific country is being presented, summarizes the main points of the viewpoint, and offers three **guided reading questions** to aid in understanding and comprehension.

- **For further discussion** questions that promote critical thinking by asking the reader to compare and contrast aspects of the viewpoints or draw conclusions about perspectives and arguments.

- A worldwide list of **organizations to contact** for readers seeking additional information.

- A **periodical bibliography** for each chapter and a **bibliography of books** on the volume topic to aid in further research.

- A comprehensive **subject index** to offer access to people, places, events, and subjects cited in the text, with the countries covered in the viewpoints highlighted.

Global Viewpoints is designed for a broad spectrum of readers who want to learn more about current events, history, political science, government, international relations, economics, environmental science, world cultures, and sociology—students doing research for class assignments or debates, teachers and faculty seeking to supplement course materials, and others wanting to understand current issues better. By presenting how people in various countries perceive the root causes, current consequences, and proposed solutions to worldwide challenges, Global Viewpoints volumes offer readers opportunities to enhance their global awareness and their knowledge of cultures worldwide.

Introduction

> "The problem of juvenile delinquency is becoming more complicated and universal, and crime prevention programmes are either unequipped to deal with the present realities or do not exist. Many developing countries have done little or nothing to deal with these problems, and international programmes are obviously insufficient."
>
> —"Juvenile Delinquency,"
> chap. 7 *in* World Youth Report 2003:
> The Global Situation of
> Young People, *United Nations*

Children were not always treated in the same way that they are today. For centuries, human life expectancy hovered around the age of forty, and teenagers and young adults were the backbone of society: People married as children or adolescents, had babies as teenagers, fought in wars, ran businesses, ruled empires and led governments, and died in what we today consider middle age. There was little emphasis on "childhood," as economic and social realities dictated that children worked long hours alongside their parents and took on adult responsibilities at a young age. In fact, the historian Philippe Ariès concluded that European societies during the Middle Ages did not accord any special status to children before the 1600s.

That philosophy toward children and adolescents was also applied to juvenile crime. During the Middle Ages, the Catholic Church determined that by the age of seven, an individual had learned right from wrong and presumed to have the use of reason. Children were treated as miniature adults, and laws did not distinguish between juvenile and adult offenses. Juvenile offenders as young as seven were tried in adult courts and incarcerated in the same institutions as adults; in fact, early jails housed children, adults, and mentally ill offenders. Children and teenagers were often victimized and exploited in such conditions.

It wasn't until the advent of the seventeenth century that the modern concept of childhood began to take hold in Western society. Cultural authorities began to discern between different age groups, and toys and literature geared toward children and adolescents became popular. Children became more dependent on their parents and stayed in school longer. Moral and intellectual figures began to write about the innocence of children and insist that they be protected from vice and the violence of the outside world. The English philosopher John Locke proposed the *tabula rasa* view of childhood, a theory that posits that children are not innately bad but are "blank tablets" who need the support and moral and ethical guidance of parents in order to grow up into law-abiding and productive members of society.

In the early years of the United States, criminal justice reformers focused on reducing overcrowding in jails and protecting children from the corruption and violence of adult offenders. In 1825 the first juvenile detention facility in the United States, known as a House of Refuge, opened in New York City. In the next few decades, fifty-three more opened around the country. These facilities also housed abandoned, orphaned, impoverished, or incorrigible children. In the mid-nineteenth century, training and industrial schools became a popular way of schooling and training young offenders for a career or skill that they could use once they were released.

In 1899 the first juvenile court in the United States was established in Chicago. The court was based on the British legal doctrine of *parens patriae*, or "the state as parent," which asserted that it was the duty of the state to act as the guardian of interests of juveniles in criminal court. The next few decades witnessed the proliferation of juvenile courts around the country, spurred by the emerging idea that children and adolescents were less culpable than adults for their crimes and could be rehabilitated. Judges were given flexibility in individual cases in order to tailor punishment according to an individual's needs, and confidentiality was established in order to avoid stigmatizing a child's reputation for the rest of his or her life.

By the 1960s, a new wave of reform swept over the US juvenile justice system. Reformers argued that juvenile criminal suspects should be afforded the same due process rights as adults. The Supreme Court agreed. As Justice Abe Fortas wrote in his opinion in *Kent v. United States* in 1966, "There is evidence, in fact, that there may be grounds for concern that the child receives the worst of both worlds: that he gets neither the protections accorded to adults nor the solicitous care and regenerative treatment postulated for children." In a series of key Supreme Court decisions, the justices ruled that juveniles must be given the same due process protections as adults, including the protection against self-incrimination and the right to counsel.

More attacks on the US juvenile justice system were launched in the 1970s, as social reformers sharply criticized the rough and inhumane treatment of juveniles in detention centers and jails. It was thought that social and community programs could better address the roots of juvenile crime—poverty, parental abuse and/or neglect, educational deficiencies, a lack of employment or educational opportunities—than dumping offenders in jail or detention centers. They successfully pushed for the passage of the Juvenile Justice and Delinquency Prevention Act in 1974, a law that orders the separate treatment of adult and juvenile offenders and created the federal Office of Juvenile Justice and Delinquency Prevention, an agency tasked with providing grants to states for developing community-based programs as alternatives to incarceration, including group homes and halfway houses.

With the sharp rise in violent crime rates in the late 1970s, the American attitude toward criminals changed. The trend of separating juvenile and adult criminals reversed and providing youth offenders special consideration became an unpopular practice. Many politicians began to push "get-tough-on-crime" legislation for both adult and juvenile offenders, and it became standard to argue that juvenile offenders should be tried in adult courts. By the 1990s, almost every state legislature in the United States had passed more punitive laws against juvenile offenders. These new laws emphasized punishment, not rehabilitation. This trend toward the punitive treatment of juveniles continues to spur controversy in the United States, as many states introduce and debate new, stringent laws for dealing with juvenile offenders.

Globally, many countries are struggling with the same issues in the fight against juvenile crime: Should the criminal justice system focus on rehabilitation and community-based programs to address the problem, or should legislators pass "tough-on-crime" laws that stress punishment?

The authors of the viewpoints presented in *Global Viewpoints: Juvenile Crime* explore some key trends emerging in juvenile crime and juvenile justice in countries around the world and assess the state of the global juvenile justice system. The information in this volume provides insight into risk factors that affect the rate of juvenile crime in some countries; outline the unique political, economical, and social challenges that some countries face in tackling juvenile crime; examine recent juvenile justice system reforms and evaluate the impact these changes have had on juvenile crime rates; and provide a glimpse of how various governments approach and deal with juvenile crime.

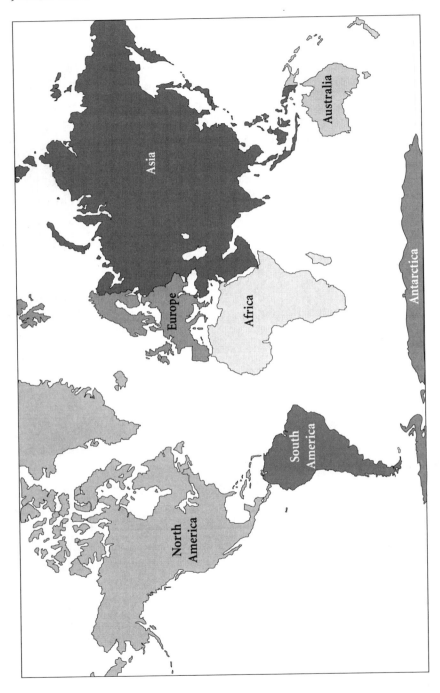

CHAPTER 1

Trends in Juvenile Crime and Punishment

The United States Has a Higher Rate of Juvenile Crime than Other Western Countries

Cully Stimson

Cully Stimson is senior legal fellow and senior policy analyst in the Center for Legal and Judicial Studies at the Heritage Foundation. In the following viewpoint, he argues that harsh treatment of American juvenile offenders is a result of the unique nature of the problem in the United States. Stimson contends that because the United States has much higher rates of violent crimes and homicides committed by juveniles than other Western nations have, stronger measures to address the problem are justified. Stimson also notes that although the United States has a higher incarceration rate, Americans convicted spend less time in prison on average than do offenders in other developed nations.

As you read, consider the following questions:

1. According to the US Department of Justice, when was the peak year in juvenile violent crime arrests?

2. How many recorded crimes were committed in the United States in 1998, according to US Department of Justice statistics?

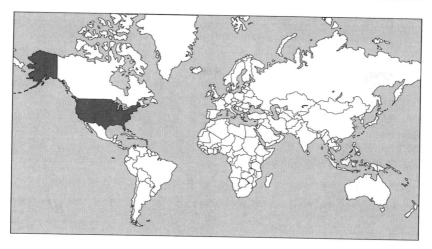

3. By how much does the author say that the US incarceration rate bests that of Russia?

Underlying nearly every argument made by opponents of life without parole for juvenile offenders is the premise that, because many other countries have not authorized or have repealed the sentence, the United States should do the same so that it can be in conformance with the international "consensus" on the matter.

Juvenile violent crime remains much higher in the United States than in other Western nations.

In fact, this premise is the cornerstone of the litigation strategy to extend the Eighth Amendment's prohibition on "cruel and unusual punishments" to reach life-without-parole sentences for juveniles. This application of foreign sources of law to determine domestic law, in addition to being legally problematic, too often overlooks the qualitative differences between the United States and other countries.

This has certainly been the case in the debate over life without parole for juvenile offenders. The leading reports on the issue do not grapple seriously with the facts concerning juvenile crime and how those facts differ between nations. Instead, they play a crude counting game, tallying up nations while ignoring the realities of their circumstances and juvenile justice systems.

The Facts on Worldwide Crime and Sentencing

The fact is that the United States faces higher rates of crimes, particularly violent crimes and homicides, than nearly any other country. Adults and juveniles commit crimes in huge numbers, from misdemeanor thefts to premeditated murders. The root causes of this epidemic have been debated, studied, tested, and analyzed for decades, but the fact of its existence is neither controversial nor in doubt.

After a decade of gains in deterring juvenile crime, the trend has turned the other way in recent years. According to the U.S. Department of Justice, there was "substantial growth in juvenile violent crime arrests ... in the late 1980s [that] peaked in 1994." Between 1994 and 2004, the arrest rate for juveniles for violent crimes fell 49 percent, only to see a 2 percent uptick in 2005 and then a 4 percent gain in 2006. In 2005 and 2006, arrests of juveniles for murder and robbery also increased.

Despite the progress made through 2004, juvenile violent crime remains much higher in the United States than in other Western nations. Some statistics:

- In 1998 alone, 24,537,600 recorded crimes were committed in the United States.

- Of the 72 countries that reported recorded crimes to the United Nations Seventh Survey of Crime Trends, the United States ranked first in total recorded crimes.

- Worse still, the United States reported more crimes than the next six countries (Germany, England/Wales, France, South Africa, Russia, and Canada) combined. Their total was 23,111,318.

- Even more tellingly, the U.S. had a higher crime rate than all of those countries, except for England, which experienced disproportionate rates of property crimes but much lower rates of violent crimes.

Juvenile Crime Statistics

In terms of violent crime rates, the U.S. ranks highly in every category, and the same is true in the realm of juvenile crime. For example:

- In 1998, teenagers in the United States were suspects in 1,609,303 crimes, and 1,000,279 juveniles were prosecuted.

- That is as many juvenile prosecutions as the next seven highest countries combined. Those countries are England/Wales, Thailand, Germany, China, Canada, Turkey, and South Korea.

- According to 2002 World Health Organization statistics, the United States ranks third in murders committed by youths and 14th in murders per capita committed by youths.

- In terms of rates, the United States is the only non-developing Western nation on the list until number 38 (New Zealand). Countries with similar youth murder rates include Panama, the Philippines, Kazakhstan, Paraguay, Cuba, and Belarus. In terms of juvenile killers per capita, the United States is more like Colombia or Mexico than the United Kingdom, which ranks 52 on the list.

US Juveniles and Crime, 2009

Most serious offense	Percent involving juveniles	
	Clearance	Arrest
Violent Crime Index	11%	15%
Property Crime Index	15	24
Murder	5	9
Forcible rape	11	14
Robbery	15	25
Aggravated assault	10	12
Burglary	15	25
Larceny-theft	18	24
Motor vehicle theft	15	24
Arson	35	44

These data come from the Federal Bureau of Investigation's *Crime in the United States 2009.*

TAKEN FROM: Charles Puzzanchera and Benjamin Adams, "Juvenile Arrests 2009," US Department of Justice, December 2011.

Incarceration Rates

Given this domestic crime problem, it should come as no great surprise that the United States tops the lists of total prisoners and prisoners per capita. The U.S. incarceration rate bests that of the runner-up, Russia, by more than 20 percent.

Despite this high incarceration rate, convicted persons in the United States actually served less time in prison, on average, than the world average and the European average. Among the 35 countries surveyed on this question in 1998, the average time actually served in prison was 32.62 months. Europeans sentenced to prison served an average of 30.89 months. Those in the United States served an average of only 28 months.

These crucial statistics are not mentioned by those who urge abolition of life-without-parole sentences for juvenile offenders. The reason may be that it undercuts their arguments: If the juvenile crime problem in the United States is not comparable to the juvenile crime problems of other Western nations, then combating it may justifiably require different, and stronger, techniques. The fact that some other nations no longer sentence juvenile offenders to life without parole loses a significant degree of its relevance. In addition, the data on sentence length demonstrate that the use of life-without-parole sentences is not a function of excessive sentence lengths in the United States, but rather an anomaly in a criminal justice system that generally imposes shorter sentences than those of other developed nations.

Balkans Grapple with Exploding Youth Crime

Sabina Niksic

Sabina Niksic is a reporter for the Agence France-Presse. In the following viewpoint, she examines the surging juvenile crime problem in Bosnia and Herzegovina, Serbia, and Croatia. Niksic points out that the issue has been neglected by the government: In Serbia and Croatia, there aren't enough funds to deal effectively with the problem, and Bosnia is hampered by simmering political squabbles and ethnic tensions. Activists are pushing for the creation of a juvenile justice system in Balkan countries as well as for a separate prison system to ensure that juvenile offenders are not housed with adult criminals, Niksic reports.

As you read, consider the following questions:

1. What percentage of 2007 crimes in Bosnia and Serbia does the author say were committed by juveniles?
2. According to a recent study of Bosnian minors, how many children aged twelve to fifteen admitted to carrying a knife or other dangerous weapon and shoplifting?
3. What is the repeat crime rate among Serbian juveniles, according to the author?

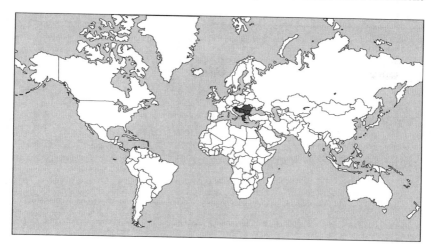

Following a decade of wars and ensuing social and economic decline, Balkan countries find themselves ill equipped to handle growing juvenile crime and delinquency. In 2007, youngsters were responsible for 10% of all known offences committed in Bosnia and Serbia, and 5% in Croatia, official statistics show. However, these rates have been surging for several years and surveys suggest the real number of law-breaking youths is significantly higher.

Serbia and Croatia have acknowledged the problem, but are handicapped by a lack of funds, while in Bosnia simmering nationalism and constant political squabbling have put the issue on the back burner. "The public only hears about the most brutal crimes committed by youngsters, but estimates of the gloomy number of juvenile crimes indicates something really bad is happening with our children," says Elmedin Muratbegović, of the Faculty of Criminal Justice in Sarajevo.

"But the government is not reacting. We have no preventive, correctional or repressive mechanisms to deal with the problem," he adds.

One in 20 Bosnian children aged 12 to 15 admits to carrying a knife or other dangerous weapon and shoplifting, according to a recent faculty study of 1,750 Bosnian minors.

Every sixth child polled had been involved in brawls, and one in 50 acknowledged that they had inflicted injuries on others that were serious enough for the victim to have sought medical attention.

Juvenile Justice

Government neglect of the problem enables youngsters to avoid punishment despite repeat offences, making them perfect recruits for seasoned criminals.

Unlike Croatia and Serbia, Bosnia lacks a special juvenile justice system, as well as prisons for minors. Its two juvenile correctional centres are below international standards. Teenage offenders thus end up in prisons with hardened criminals.

"We are very concerned about that," says Hubert van Eck Koster, human rights officer with the Bosnian mission of the Organisation for Security and Co-operation in Europe. "If you have a juvenile in the same prison cell with a suspected war criminal, which we have seen happen, that is clearly not helpful."

However, a recent string of high-profile incidents involving youths has caused an upsurge in public anger over the problem, putting the government under pressure to make the problem a priority. In February, thousands protested in Sarajevo against government inaction following the death of a 17-year-old boy who was beaten and stabbed in a tram by three teenage boys.

The incident came just a couple of weeks after a 72-year-old woman died from burns when her head was splashed with petrol and set alight by three boys aged 15 to 16. One suspect reportedly had committed 128 criminal acts in 2007. He was among 91 of 93 minors who were repeat offenders released in Sarajevo last year.

The government has since enforced a so-called national strategy for juvenile offending, which won parliamentary approval in 2006 but has been left waiting promulgation. It fore-

---

It Is Time to Act in the Federation of Bosnia and Herzegovina

Back in the Federation of Bosnia and Herzegovina, it seems prosecutors, judges, police officers and social workers are only just beginning to grapple with a problem that has vexed most European states for years: balancing the needs and rights of juvenile offenders against the well-being of the rest of society.

In June this year [2011], Ramiz Kadić, deputy mayor of Sarajevo, told a roomful of youth crime professionals attending a conference on juvenile offending that it was time to act.

"We, as a society, cannot excuse ourselves by blaming the war for everything we have not done. Those times have passed by and we must go for social reform," he says.

As in all countries, failure to address youth crime does not only mean states have failed their children, but they have compromised the future too.

Ahmed Burić,
"Federation Fails to Curb Rising Bosnian Youth Crime,"
Balkan Insight, November 9, 2011.

---

sees the implementation of preventative programmes similar to those which have already proved a success in Serbia, where they were introduced at schools about four years ago.

"Already after a year, violent and undisciplined behavior . . . has visibly reduced among schoolchildren," says Branislava Popović-Ćitić, from the Faculty for Special Education and Rehabilitation in Belgrade.

Repeat Crimes

However, repeat crime rates among Serbian juveniles still remain very high at between 40% and 60%. "Juvenile criminals are somewhat neglected because the authorities struggle with rampant adult crime," says Professor Vladimir Krivokapić, once a justice minister in the former Yugoslavia. "But the failure to successfully deal with young offenders creates the danger they will embark on careers of criminality."

Popović-Ćitić blames the problem on a shortage of resources. "But due to permanent work on the problem and strong efforts to build a wide social coalition to fight against it, I believe it could change in the future," she says.

Croatia in 2006 adopted a national action plan for the protection of rights of children, including measures to fight against juvenile criminal offences.

"It proves the awareness of the problem is high but important measures remain 'empty words' due to the lack of funding for their implementation," says Mila Jelavić, Croatia's ombudsperson for children.

Bosnia is described by some as the perfect breeding ground for young criminals.

However, experts in Bosnia say funding is the least of the country's problems when it comes to juvenile delinquency.

"Even the simplest incidents in Bosnia are politicised," says psychology professor Vladimir Obradović, who conducted one of the first studies of risk behaviours among teenagers and case studies of juvenile criminals.

"When serious crimes occur, media immediately focus on ethnicity of criminals and their victims, setting the stage for politicians and their nationalist rhetoric," he says.

Bosnia is described by some as the perfect breeding ground for young criminals. This is explained by its ethnically fragmented education system, half of the population living below or close to the poverty line, omnipresent ethnic tensions and public glorification of war criminals and transition profiteers.

"I believe that we are now only seeing the tip of the iceberg. I am afraid to even just think about what hides below the surface," sociologist Mirsad Abazović emphasises.

British Rates of Girl Gang Crime Are Exploding

Paul Bracchi

Paul Bracchi is a reporter for the Daily Mail. *In the following viewpoint, he explores the rising trend of violent girl gangs in England. Bracchi reports that these gangs are responsible for a series of heinous, violent acts against innocent people and often involve young girls, casual sexual activity, and brutal fights with other gangs. Most of these girls join for protection and camaraderie, live in poor neighborhoods, and come from broken homes, reports Bracchi. Another factor in the rise of girl gangs, asserts the author, is the coarsening of British culture, which seems to celebrate bad behavior.*

As you read, consider the following questions:

1. According to a Home Office report, how much have crimes committed by girls as young as ten risen from 2005 to 2008?
2. How many girl gangs are there in London, according to a police estimate?
3. What does the author say is the most common age of juvenile females convicted in the courts in England?

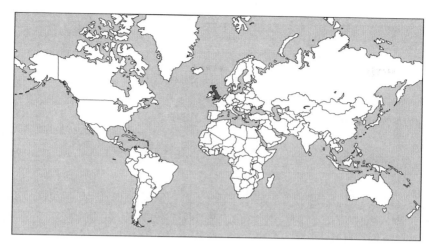

The girl emerged from her house with a mobile phone glued to her ear and a cigarette hanging out of her mouth.

Her friends take the mickey out of her [make fun of her], we learn from her sister's MySpace Internet page, because she is never out of "a chav T-shirt and tracksuit bottoms"—and she didn't disappoint yesterday.

Even so, it doesn't pay to get on the wrong side of this 14-year-old, who plays for a local girls' football team and weighs in at around 13 stone.

Someone who did is retired schoolteacher Beryl Barber.

A Vicious Attack

The pensioner was walking along the pavement near her home in Selby, North Yorkshire, recently when she was confronted by the girl in question and her "mates".

The gang (three girls, two boys) fancied the odds: five of them versus one defenceless 72-year-old woman.

They began hurling stones at Mrs Barber. She could have turned away, as many in her position would have done. In-stead, however, she picked up one of the stones and threw it back.

The retaliation was swift and sadistic.

Suddenly, the girl rushed towards Mrs Barber and pushed her into the path of an oncoming car which had to brake sharply to avoid a collision.

Nevertheless, Mrs Barber fell with such force that, in the words of an eyewitness, "her face literally bounced off the pavement, skidding across the tarmac."

Mrs Barber suffered a broken nose and two black eyes, and was left looking like the girl had played football—with her head.

The girl's motive, according to the police, was to make her "look good" in front of her group; to gain "respect".

It is a word that features prominently in the street lingo of such youngsters, and never was it more misplaced.

The girl, the second of three children who lives with her parents on the outskirts of Selby, was given a 12-month referral order when she appeared before magistrates in March 2008; the equivalent, many might think, of a "slap on the wrist".

Under the terms of the order she has to attend a course in anger management.

That is as much as we are allowed to tell you about her, because in the eyes of the law she is still a juvenile.

Mrs Barber, for her part, was too scared to come to the door when we called at her bungalow.

A Disturbing Trend

This is the reality behind a Home Office [government department] report this week [in May 2008] which revealed that crimes committed by girls as young as ten have soared by 25 per cent in three years.

The statistics mask an even more disturbing trend.

Many of these feral females are involved in gangs.

Be they all-girl gangs, mixed gangs (like the one which targeted Beryl Barber) or male gangs to which they become attached.

Sometimes beneath a cap or a "hoodie" it is hard to tell one sex from another anymore—girl from boy, or boy from girl.

Either way, in this *Clockwork Orange* world [referring to a dystopian novella by Anthony Burgess], pushing a pensioner into a road, or mugging an innocent passer-by, earns you respect.

Two further incidents in the past few weeks alone highlight the frightening escalation of the kind of female gang violence which, until recently, was presented as an intrinsically male problem.

Sometimes beneath a cap or a "hoodie" it is hard to tell one sex from another anymore—girl from boy, or boy from girl.

One was at Shoreham railway station, near Brighton, when about 20 girls—from two rival gangs—fought a pitched battle on the platform with beer bottles and snooker balls wrapped in socks. Two girls, aged 18 and 20, have been charged with affray [fighting].

The other occurred in the Midlands, where a woman was mercilessly punched, kicked, and stamped on by a mob of teenage girls who, she says, acted "like a pack of wild animals".

You do not have to grow up on a sink estate, come from a broken home, get excluded from school, be promiscuous, binge drink or play violent computer games to become immersed in this culture.

But—boy or girl—this is more likely if you do.

The most recent Metropolitan Police estimate put the number of gangs in London at 174, of which at least three were exclusively girls.

But the report concedes: "The actual number could be even greater as this is based purely on police intelligence."

Among the girl "crews" believed to [be] operating in the capital today are the "Shower Gyals" (Tottenham), PYG (Peckham), identified by black bandanas, and OCS (Brixton), which is said to have members as young as ten.

Last year, a running feud between the PYG and OCS turned into a mass brawl in Camberwell, South London.

Such girls, according to a study to be published by the Centre for Policy Studies next month, routinely carry knives and "are prepared to use them".

You do not have to . . . come from a broken home, get excluded from school, be promiscuous, binge drink or play violent computer games to become immersed in this culture.

Initiation rites might require a girl to rob or mug.

Casual sex ("linking") is endemic and videos of girls and boys having sex in the stairwells of housing blocks circulate school playgrounds.

London, where the research was conducted, is the norm, not the exception.

The NG2 Crew

In Nottingham there is the NG2 Crew, for example, an all-girl gang named after the postcode which includes the notorious Meadows estate, a crime-ridden warren of dimly lit council houses.

Becki, 16, lives with her mother—her father has long since gone—in the area.

Many of her peers come from the Meadows. Her brother is a drug dealer, selling "skunk" cannabis.

Becki is a member of the NG2.

"I have been part of the crew for six months now," she said last night.

"It's like a type of protection. My mum works all the time [in a supermarket] so I hardly ever see her and there is no one at home, so I don't feel I have anyone looking after me really.

"I started hanging out with the girls from school and we just decided to form a crew."

It sounds innocent enough until Becki admits: "It gets serious when arguments start. One of our girls had a 'beef' with another girl from a different area and when that happened we had to protect her and help her to sort it out.

"We went round and beat the other girl up.

"We punched her and we also took off our shoes and hit her with them. It was like a warning really that they should not mess with us.

For some young girls, joining a male gang is their way of trying to feel cool, desirable and protected.

"A lot of rows are over boys, or it's name-calling and girls showing us disrespect.

"We stand up for one another. It's like having a big family. You feel safe. You can go anywhere as long as your girls are with you."

A Degenerating Culture

What's clear is that there has been a dramatic coarsening in the behaviour of an entire underclass of young women—driven partly by the destruction of the nuclear family and the lack of a strong father figure, but also by a celebrity culture in which female so-called "stars"—famous only for appearing on *Big Brother* or its equivalents—are photographed blind drunk and fighting in the gutter with other women outside nightclubs.

For some young girls, joining a male gang is their way of trying to feel cool, desirable and protected.

The Role of Gender in Gang Violence

Susan Batchelor, at the Scottish Centre for Crime and Justice Research at the University of Glasgow, has done several studies on girls and violence and points out that female gang members are still a rarity—their male counterparts commit 80% of all gang-related crimes. It is important not to over-emphasise girls' violence—but it does help to recognise that gender plays a large part in criminal identity, and is potentially the key to helping people change. "Powerlessness defines the experiences of most young women who turn violent. . . . The women's movement has not reached their consciousness."

Angela Neustatter, "Blood Sisters," Guardian, *July 3, 2008.*

The price for such protection—and the material rewards of membership—are high.

Such girls are known as "bitches".

"In Leeds, every postcode and every little area has its own crew," says Pat Regan, who runs a Mothers Against Violence group in the city.

There's the Hyde Park Crew, the Little London Crew, and the CPT from Chapeltown. All these gangs have girls in them.

They see the boys in nice clothes and driving flash cars and they want a part of it.

"But nothing is free. The girls often have to keep guns and drugs for their so-called boyfriends, who will usually have several girls on the go, and they end up with the convictions when they are caught."

Violence, in one way or another, defines these girls. The underlying evidence, if anyone cared to look, has been there for some time.

The most common age of a female criminal—calculated from the average age of juvenile females convicted in the courts—has fallen to just 14.

In the early nineties, the age was 16.

Equally disturbing is the shift towards thuggery.

The figures released by the Youth Justice Board [for England and Wales] on Thursday, as the *Mail* reported yesterday, show significant increases in assaults, robberies and public order offences.

It was 8pm on a sunny April evening when Wendy Clarke, a 47-year-old mother from the Birmingham suburbs, got caught up in this nightmare world. She had just locked up her tanning salon when she spotted a group of about 20 girls congregating near a bus shelter.

Four of the gang—although she didn't know they were a gang at the time—were sitting near an elderly man on a bench. "They began taunting him," says Wendy.

"Grandad", they called him. One of the girls then opened his jacket and started rummaging through his pockets.

"Soon they were all over him like a pack of animals and I knew I had to do something."

The Price of Intervention

She strode over to the group and told them to "back off and leave him alone".

Almost before the words had left her mouth, one of the girls yanked her by the hair and punched her in the face. Two others jumped on her back.

Three more joined in and jumped on Wendy's head when she fell to the ground.

"One minute I was telling them to leave the man alone and the next I was on the floor," she says.

"During the attack I was aware of more and more girls joining in. I tried my best to defend myself, but it was useless. I was completely and utterly helpless.

"All the time they were shouting abuse and baying like savages. It was absolutely terrifying and I thought it would never end."

Wendy might not have got out alive if a couple hadn't pulled up in their car and run over to help when they realised what was happening, causing Wendy's attackers to flee.

It would be [a] mistake to think this was a spontaneous, random attack. True, the girls did not know who their victim was going to be, but they knew they were going to get someone.

They were wearing several layers of clothing so they could change their appearance quickly. Unfortunately for them, someone followed them to a nearby McDonald's and dialled 999 [emergency phone number in the United Kingdom]. The girls were in the process of "undressing" when officers arrived.

Ten girls, aged between 14 and 17, were later arrested and bailed in connection with the attack on Wendy.

Her injuries were so severe that doctors couldn't be certain whether her nose had been broken until the swelling had gone down.

"My boyfriend didn't recognise me when he saw me," she said.

"I have a 15-year-old daughter and the difference between her and 'them' is difficult to comprehend."

Brutal Bullies Are Brought to Justice

Consider, too, the harrowing experience of an 18-year-old youth, whom we shall call Ben, who agreed to meet us in a park in Woolwich, southeast London this week.

Ben went to live with foster parents following a deeply troubled upbringing (his father committed suicide) which has left him with severe emotional problems.

He is also partially disabled after injuring his legs in a motorbike accident.

All in all, it would be difficult to find a more vulnerable teenager.

Ben, who is slightly built, was walking down the street, near the spot where he is now standing, one day last year when he was ambushed by a gang of five girls.

The girls supplied cannabis to Ben's cousin. When his cousin left a drug debt unpaid, they took revenge on Ben instead.

The group, aged 15 and 16, dragged him into a nearby flat where they stripped him, repeatedly beat him with a broken broom handle, and made him perform sex acts.

They filmed his three-and-a-half-hour ordeal on a mobile phone.

"I did not fight back because there were at least five of them and they were stronger than me. I pleaded with them to stop but they wouldn't. I just covered my face."

Initially, Ben was too embarrassed to go to the police. "They were girls, after all," he said.

Had his sister not eventually persuaded him to inform the authorities, his story would have been difficult to believe. He gave evidence against the gang via video link because he was too embarrassed to face them in court.

The girls were convicted for false imprisonment, assault, and causing a person to engage in sexual activity without consent. They were jailed for a total of nine years at Inner London Crown Court.

The judge called the attack "sadistic" and "disgraceful".

The background of the girls, who again cannot be identified, provides chilling insight into the culture of female violence and girl gangs.

One had a previous conviction for assault. When she was just 13 she punched another girl in the face, fracturing her cheekbone, leaving her needing a metal plate.

She was skilled in martial arts and her CV [history] included robbery and threatening and abusive behaviour. Two of her accomplices also had previous convictions for crimes including robbery, assault and drug offences.

These are the kind of nihilistic, violent crimes, of course, that we used to associate with men not women, boys not girls.

The truth is there is little difference anymore—which is perhaps the most shocking indictment of all.

Some Central American Countries Treat Youth Gang Crime as a Threat to Regional Security

Peter Peetz

Peter Peetz is a political scientist and research fellow at the German Institute of Global and Area Studies. In the following viewpoint, he analyzes the connection between public discourse on the problem of youth violence and related governmental policies in Costa Rica, El Salvador, and Nicaragua. Peetz finds that El Salvadoran policies on youth crime are harsh and repressive because the discourse portrays youth violence as a serious threat to national security. In Nicaragua and Costa Rica, he reports, juvenile crime policies are not as repressive because the discourse is more measured and balanced. El Salvador's approach is particularly troubling because it has worked to demonize a whole generation of young people, Peetz maintains.

As you read, consider the following questions:

1. According to Peetz, what percentage of the Latin American population is under the age of fifteen?
2. How does the author define *mara*?

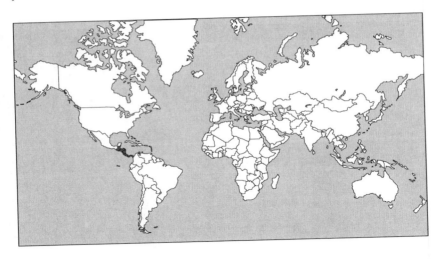

3. How do governments and other actors utilize the term
   seguridad ciudadana?

Within the policy and research field of violence, crime,
and insecurity in Latin America, analysts increasingly
see violent and criminal behavior among youths as a crucial
topic. In many countries, youth violence is identified as one
major cause of insecurity. In addition to the concerns raised
from a mere security perspective, social actors and scholars
focus on youth violence from other viewpoints as well; they
discuss it, for instance, with regard to social and development
policies. As approximately one-third of the Latin American
population is under 15 years of age, social phenomena among
youths are highly relevant to the present and future development of the region's societies. On the other hand, in the field
of violence and security studies, interest in the different phenomena, causes, and consequences of youth violence began to
boom when the debate on violence in Latin America shifted
its main focus from political to criminal and social violence;
that is, from guerrilla warfare, state terrorism, and "dirty
wars" to street delinquency, organized crime, gang violence,
domestic violence, vigilante justice, and so forth. In this con-

text, youth violence gains importance as an issue interrelated with many other problems: youths and petty crime, youths in gangs, violent youths as (former) victims of domestic violence, youths and drugs, etc. By far the most prominent youth-violence phenomenon in Latin America is the Central American—more exactly the Guatemalan, Salvadoran, and Honduran—*maras*, a special type of youth gang that originated in the context of emigration to and deportation from the US.

This [viewpoint] argues that in some countries of Central America—and presumably in other parts of Latin America—specific groups of young people and, to a certain degree, the younger generation as a whole are socially constructed as a threat to citizen security (*seguridad ciudadana*). In particular, the members of youth gangs (*maras*) are constructed as the number-one menace to the security of the whole of Central America. In this vein, the persecution of youths in the name of *seguridad ciudadana* is legitimized and justified.

A Threat to Citizen Security

All over Latin America, government policies meant to prevent and/or combat youth violence are generally designed and implemented within the context of the state's policies of *seguridad ciudadana*. The concrete meaning of *seguridad ciudadana* varies significantly, depending on who uses it (and where, when, etc.). However, many authors agree that the term relates to two levels of reality. First, it refers to a condition or a state: to the absence of threats which could endanger the security of a person or a group. In this sense, the term has a highly normative meaning. It describes an ideal situation—probably inexistent in any part of the world but existing "*como un objetivo a perseguir*" ("as an objective to strive for"). Second, it refers to public policies aiming (but probably never managing) to achieve this ideal situation. In other words, it refers to policies that seek to eliminate security threats or to protect the population vis-à-vis these threats. In this latter sense, the term *seguridad ciudadana* refers to an empirically existent social practice.

Governments and other actors use the term *seguridad ciudadana* because it has the connotation of a preventive and, to a certain degree, liberal approach to problems of violence and crime. The expression as such emphasizes the protection of the citizen. It thus contrasts with the protection and defense of the state as postulated by the concept of *seguridad nacional* (national security), which dominated the public debate on security in past decades. The terminological shift suggests that the state now protects the physical integrity, property, and individual rights of all citizens. Yet, the concept and practice of *seguridad ciudadana* tend to create a difference between citizens who deserve protection and social groups considered to be a potential threat. Depending on the country, the latter may be, for example, drug addicts or dealers, ethnic groups, immigrants, or, as this [viewpoint] argues, youths. In a way, people who are part of these groups become the "criminal other" because the policies of *seguridad ciudadana* implicitly exclude them. Often, the state does not protect these people, and their human and civil rights are violated. This, in turn, is justified by the alleged need to protect those citizens considered to deserve protection.

The Discourse on Youth Crime and Security Varies

In the three countries analyzed, the public discourse on youth violence can be summarized as a mixture of viewpoints locatable on a continuum between favoring repression on the one hand, and advocating preventive, rehabilitation and human rights–based policies on the other. Every country has a specific "mix ratio" of these viewpoints, Nicaragua being located rather on the non-repressive side, Costa Rica somewhere in the middle, and El Salvador on the more repressive side. But neither in Nicaragua nor in El Salvador can the discourses be described as purely non-repressive or purely repressive. In Nicaragua and Costa Rica, where the social discourse on youth violence—compared to El Salvador—is less prominent in the public debate and less homogeneous between powerful and not so powerful speakers, the state policies are neither very accentuated nor very coherent, whether in terms of repressive or non-repressive measures. In El Salvador, the state's response to youth violence and juvenile delinquency coincides with a generalized public fear regarding these phenomena. This congruence also applies to particular aspects of youth crime policy. One example of this is the shift in the depiction of youth gangs (in the media and government discourse) from a youth culture problem to one of organized crime, parallel to a corresponding shift in the authorities' strategies to combat the gangs.

In El Salvador youths in general are socially constructed as a potential threat to security. Youth gang members in particular are constructed as the "criminal others" from whom society has to be protected by means of specific *seguridad ciudadana* policies. The same might also apply in the cases of Guatemala and Honduras, which appear to be similar to El Salvador, but (because of the limited geographical scope of the sources analyzed for this [viewpoint]) this cannot be substantiated here. For Nicaragua and Costa Rica, neither social discourse nor governmental policies suggest that adolescents in general are being stigmatized as a security threat. A closer look at the sources would be necessary, though, to check if there are particular groups of young people, for example young drug addicts, young immigrants, etc., who are systematically constructed as the dangerous "other." In any case, it seems that in Nicaragua and Costa Rica there are other characteristics than simply "being young" that turn a person into a source of fear and an object of security policies. Nevertheless, *maras* are constructed as an imminent (Costa Rica) or only

The Impact of Juvenile Violence on Central America

Gang activity in Central America poses an increasing threat to the security of the region and the safety of its citizens, particularly in El Salvador, Guatemala, and Honduras. The problem is exacerbated by high levels of youth unemployment along with insufficient access to education and economic opportunities, inadequate social services, family disintegration and inter-familial violence, and overwhelmed and ineffective justice systems. High levels of crime affect Central Americans' psychosocial well-being and that of their families. Extortion associated with violent crime has shattered communities and their ability to coexist. Neighbors lack trust in one another and in government institutions who must increasingly divert resources away from economic growth for the purposes of combating crime and violence.

"Regional Youth Alliance for Gang Violence Prevention,"
United States Agency for International Development (USAID),
August 16, 2011.

possible (Nicaragua) threat, and the governments of both countries have taken part in an increasing number of regional and international initiatives to fight the gangs.

Different Approaches

The analysis of the three countries as individual cases and as a "bounded system" has provided differentiated insight into the discourse on youth violence in Central America. Given the uncontested prominence of the *mara* issue in the region's (youth) violence debate, the focus of most of the relevant literature lies on El Salvador, Guatemala, and Honduras, the countries with a massive *mara* presence and with crime and violence problems perceived as high. This [viewpoint] has taken Costa Rica and Nicaragua fully into account and has shown that even in one of these "non-*mara* countries," Costa Rica, the discourse on youth violence is an important topic in some discursive spaces, although not as important as in El Salvador. Thus, it is not necessarily the presence of youth gangs that draws public attention to the issue of youth violence. Moreover, as the depiction of *maras* as an imminent or future threat in Costa Rica and Nicaragua shows, the youth gang problem—or, more exactly, the discourse regarding it—in one part of the "bounded system" has produced significant effects on the way youth violence is discursively treated in other parts of the system.

It seems fruitful, not only for Central America but also for other Latin American countries, to emphasize the social discourse on violence and crime while researching public policies that address these problems.

On the basis of the sources analyzed in this [viewpoint], it is not possible to draw conclusions concerning *causal* relations between discourse and policies. However, the analysis suggests that there is a strong relation and mutual influence between the public's fear (or disregard) of youth violence and the state's policies to reduce that kind of violence. Based on the explorative findings of the qualitative research presented in this [viewpoint], it is possible and necessary to conduct more and differently designed research to determine what the causal linkages between discourse and policy in the field of youth violence in Central America are. Also, further research efforts should be undertaken to discover why, how, and by whom the discourses are originally generated and what the power relations which cause them to become hegemonic—and relevant in the policy-making process—are. This kind of "archaeology" would help in understanding the deeper roots of anti-youth-crime policies which in some countries, such as El Salvador, tend to disregard human and children's rights.

The Influence of Social Discourse

Overall, it seems fruitful, not only for Central America but also for other Latin American countries, to emphasize the social discourse on violence and crime while researching public policies that address these problems. The concept of *seguridad ciudadana* is not specific to Central America; it is present and relevant all through Latin America. In each context, there may be other groups of citizens marked by society as the "criminal others" from whom society has to be protected, be they immigrants, ethnic minorities, a specific age group, drug consumers, football fans, or whoever. In this [viewpoint], it has been shown that one of these demonized groups can be a whole generation, as in El Salvador. Political and social actors across Latin America should be aware that such "intergenerational apartheid" has damaging effects for democracy, human rights, and development in the region. They should design policies not only to prevent juvenile delinquency and youth violence—as states and civic organizations increasingly do—but also to prevent societies from defining their own adolescents as a threat to the citizens' security.

In Europe, Juvenile Crime Is Increasingly Prominent in the Public Consciousness

Jennifer Abramsohn

Jennifer Abramsohn is a reporter for Deutsche Welle. In the following viewpoint, she reviews the debate in different European countries over how to approach juvenile crime, particularly punishment for youth offenders. For example, Germany favors rehabilitation over incarceration and has a later age of criminal responsibility, which is the age a young criminal suspect can be tried as an adult. In Britain, Abramsohn asserts, juvenile crime policies are much tougher and the age of criminal responsibility is much lower than in other European countries.

As you read, consider the following questions:

1. According to the author, what is the age of criminal responsibility in Germany?
2. What is the age of criminal responsibility in England?
3. What does the author say happens to children under age fourteen who commit major crimes in Germany?

The crime stole headlines across Britain and around the world: In Liverpool, Robert Thompson and Jon Venables brutally tortured a two-year-old boy, James Bulger, to death.

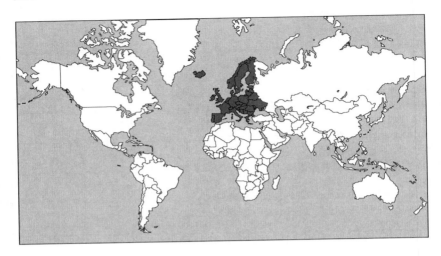

Shockingly, the perpetrators were just 10 years old. And that revelation was followed by another shock: the child perpetrators were to be tried as adults for their actions.

But as controversial as the 1996 trial was, it had almost faded into obscurity, until earlier this month [March 2010], when news broke that Venables—who had served out his sentence and was living under an assumed identity—had been arrested once again, this time for breaking the terms of his parole.

The Debate over Justice for Minors

The case has reignited a public debate in Britain over how best to deal with young offenders, and raises questions about the appropriate age for them to face justice, and the value of rehabilitation versus punishment.

A recent case in Germany has brought similar issues to light. Earlier this month, two 13-year-old boys were found to have gruesomely tortured an 83-year-old Munich woman.

The pair forced Edeltraud B., who suffers from dementia, to drink a half liter of schnapps. They beat her, sprayed shaving cream into her mouth, poured spices in her eyes and urinated on her while she lay on the ground.

The torment is believed to have lasted "for several hours," chief detective Frank Hellwig told reporters at the time.

Unlike James Bulger, Edeltraud B. survived. And there is another difference: in contrast to Venables and Thompson, the teens from Munich won't be tried for their actions. In Germany, children under age 14 are not considered criminally accountable.

The difference emphasizes the gaps among some European countries when it comes to dealing with young offenders—and with attitudes towards crime and punishment in general.

England has the lowest age of criminal responsibility in Europe—10 years. In most other European states, that age—which determines when a child can go to trial—is set at 14.

Age Limit Alone Is Not Decisive

Germany is "somewhere in the middle when you compare European countries," says Torsten Verrel, a professor in the department of criminology and juvenile justice at the University of Bonn.

However, Verrel said, the age limit for trials alone doesn't measure how well a country deals with juvenile justice.

"There are lots of other differences. Not just whether or not they put youths on trial, but other things, like the harshness of the sentencing or what other options are available."

England's law that 10-year-olds can stand trial "is extreme," Verrel said.

Dieter Doelling, a professor at the Institute of Criminology at the University of Heidelberg, agrees. By age 14 "kids can generally say they know what they were doing" when they commit a crime, Doelling asserts.

Help, Not Punishment, Is the Goal

"The younger [the perpetrators] get, the harder it gets to say if they could decide between right and wrong, and—this is also important—whether or not they were masters of their own actions."

Germany has a multitiered system when it comes to trying juveniles. Children under age 14 who commit major crimes aren't sent to trial—but they can be dealt with by psychiatric or youth services organizations. Between the ages of 14 and 18, youths are tried according to a juvenile penal code, which has milder punishments. From 18 to 21, offenders are considered young adults, which also affects sentencing.

For offenders under 14, "the basic idea is to get help for the child, rather than punishment," says Lukas Pieplow, a Cologne-based defense attorney who specializes in juvenile offenders.

Pieplow believes the system works well because it looks at each offender as an individual, taking their background and psychological testing into account, and—unlike in the case of offenders over age 21—provides individual sentencing.

"There are a lot of possibilities that grown-up offenders don't have, such as training courses, social-service care situations or taking part in a public works project" as a punishment, he said.

"In general, the system has proved to be a good one. I wouldn't want to change it," he added.

The reemergence of [violent news stories] has led many observers to ask whether society hasn't simply reached a new level of depravity that requires an all-new punishment structure.

Social Services Lacking in Funds

That kind of intensive help for youth who have gone off the tracks, or who seem to be headed there, is exactly what everyday young offenders need, the experts agreed. But they also said that funding for youth services in Germany often fails to meet society's needs.

"There is in fact a real problem when it comes to treatment," said Doelling of the University of Heidelberg.

"Many of these children should be treated in their own homes, but there isn't enough money. Program funding for social retraining courses is very uneven across the country, and there are big gaps where help is available and where it is not," he said.

Germany is making a grave mistake by failing to allocate spending to youth services, Pieplow added.

"It would be an investment in the future. Prisons are expensive, and we have to see to it that young offenders don't spend their lives in prison. When they are young, we can still set a new course," Pieplow said.

The reemergence of the Bulger case into the news, timed so closely with the horrifying story of the Munich pensioner, has led many observers to ask whether society hasn't simply reached a new level of depravity that requires an all-new punishment structure.

What's more, they worry about an overall rise in brutal youth crime, and what that would say about "civilized" European society.

Crime Statistics Are Unchanged

But according to statistics, experts say, there is no need to worry. The numbers of reported youth crimes are in fact "stagnant or going down," University of Bonn's Verrel said.

And Doelling agreed, saying that reported youth crime rose through the 1890s and into the early 1900s, but since then it has remained stable. "There is no statistical growth, if you look at the whole of juvenile offenders," he said.

The problem may possibly be that society's reaction to youth crime overall has changed, Verrel said: "In earlier times, people would just turn a blind eye. They said, 'Kids will be kids, and we'll deal with this within the community.' I can imagine that people have become more ready to press charges against children."

By far, most youth crime consists of small offenses, Verrel added. The big difference today is that the media attention on the truly appalling crimes—which have always existed in small numbers—has grown much more intense and widespread.

The United States Is Criminalizing Typical Childhood Behavior

Chris McGreal

Chris McGreal is a reporter for the Guardian. *In the following viewpoint, he argues that US schools in Texas are criminalizing normal childhood behavior by harshly penalizing kids for things like swearing or wearing inappropriate clothing. Schools also have police patrolling hallways, issuing tickets, and enforcing rules. Although authorities justify such policies and tough punishments as a necessary tool for teachers and administrators, activists are concerned that there is a "school-to-prison pipeline" being established for problem kids and that these policies allow teachers to shirk responsibility when it comes to maintaining discipline in their classrooms.*

As you read, consider the following questions:

1. According to the author, how many Class C misdemeanor tickets were issued to children as young as six in Texas for offenses in and out of school in 2010?

2. What does McGreal cite as the most frequent offense committed by Texas schoolchildren?

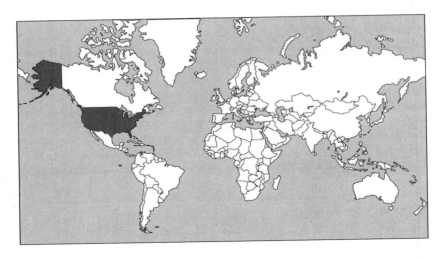

3. According to the organization Texas Appleseed, how many tickets were issued to children in primary school over the past six years in Texas?

The charge on the police docket was "disrupting class". But that's not how 12-year-old Sarah Bustamantes saw her arrest for spraying two bursts of perfume on her neck in class because other children were bullying her with taunts of "you smell".

"I'm weird. Other kids don't like me," said Sarah, who has been diagnosed with attention-deficit and bipolar disorders and who is conscious of being overweight. "They were saying a lot of rude things to me. Just picking on me. So I sprayed myself with perfume. Then they said: 'Put that away, that's the most terrible smell I've ever smelled.' Then the teacher called the police."

The policeman didn't have far to come. He patrols the corridors of Sarah's school, Fulmore Middle [School] in Austin, Texas. Like hundreds of schools in the state, and across large parts of the rest of the US, Fulmore Middle has its own police force with officers in uniform who carry guns to keep order in the canteens, playgrounds and lessons. Sarah was taken from class, charged with a criminal misdemeanour and ordered to appear in court.

Each day, hundreds of schoolchildren appear before courts in Texas charged with offences such as swearing, misbehaving on the school bus or getting into a punch-up in the playground. Children have been arrested for possessing cigarettes, wearing "inappropriate" clothes and being late for school.

In 2010, the police gave close to 300,000 "Class C misdemeanour" tickets to children as young as six in Texas for offences in and out of school, which result in fines, community service and even prison time. What was once handled with a telling-off by the teacher or a call to parents can now result in arrest and a record that may cost a young person a place in college or a job years later.

Reassessing Policy

"We've taken childhood behaviour and made it criminal," said Kady Simpkins, a lawyer who represented Sarah Bustamantes. "They're kids. Disruption of class? Every time I look at this law I think: Good lord, I never would have made it in school in the US. I grew up in Australia and it's just rowdy there. I don't know how these kids do it, how they go to school every day without breaking these laws."

The British government is studying the American experience in dealing with gangs, unruly young people and juvenile justice in the wake of the riots in England. The UK's [United Kingdom's] justice minister, Crispin Blunt, visited Texas last September [2011] to study juvenile courts and prisons, youth gangs and police outreach in schools, among other things. But his trip came at a time when Texas is reassessing its own reaction to fears of feral youth that critics say has created a "school-to-prison pipeline". The Texas Supreme Court chief justice, Wallace Jefferson, has warned that "charging kids with

61

criminal offences for low-level behavioural issues" is helping to drive many of them to a life in jail.

The Texas state legislature last year changed the law to stop the issuing of tickets to 10- and 11-year-olds over classroom behaviour. (In the state, the age of criminal responsibility is 10.) But a broader bill to end the practice entirely—championed by a state senator, John Whitmire, who called the system "ridiculous"—failed to pass and cannot be considered again for another two years.

The emphasis on law and order in the classroom parallels more than two decades of rapid expansion of all areas of policing in Texas in response to misplaced fears across the US in the 1980s of a looming crime wave.

Even the federal government has waded in, with the US attorney general, Eric Holder, saying of criminal citations being used to maintain discipline in schools: "That is something that clearly has to stop."

As almost every parent of a child drawn in to the legal labyrinth by school policing observes, it wasn't this way when they were young.

A Rising Hysteria

The emphasis on law and order in the classroom parallels more than two decades of rapid expansion of all areas of policing in Texas in response to misplaced fears across the US in the 1980s of a looming crime wave stoked by the crack epidemic, alarmist academic studies and the media.

"It's very much tied in with some of the hyperbole around the rise in juvenile crime rate that took place back in the early 90s," said Deborah Fowler, deputy director of Texas Appleseed, an Austin legal rights group, and principal author of a 200-page study of the consequences of policing in Texas schools.

"They ushered in tough, punitive policies. It was all part of the tough-on-crime movement."

Part of that included the passing of laws that made the US the only developed country to lock up children as young as 13 for life without the possibility of parole, often as accomplices to murders committed by an adult.

As the hand of law and order grew heavier across Texas, its grip also tightened on schools. The number of school districts in the state with police departments has risen more than twentyfold over the past two decades.

"Zero tolerance started out as a term that was used in combating drug trafficking and it became a term that is now used widely when you're referring to some very punitive school discipline measures. Those two policy worlds became conflated with each other," said Fowler.

In the midst of that drive came the 1999 Columbine High School massacre, in which two students in Colorado shot dead 12 other pupils and a teacher before killing themselves. Parents clamoured for someone to protect their children and police in schools seemed to many to be the answer.

But most schools do not face any serious threat of violence and police officers patrolling the corridors and canteens are largely confronted with little more than boisterous or disrespectful childhood behaviour.

Disorderly Behaviour and the Penalties

"What we see often is a real overreaction to behaviour that others would generally think of as just childish misbehaviour rather than law breaking," said Fowler. Tickets are most frequently issued by school police for "disruption of class", which can mean causing problems during lessons but is also defined as disruptive behaviour within 500ft (150 metres) of school property such as shouting, which is classified as "making an unreasonable noise".

Among the more extreme cases documented by Appleseed is of a teacher who had a pupil arrested after the child responded to a question as to where a word could be found in a text by saying: "In your *culo* (arse)", making the other children laugh. Another pupil was arrested for throwing paper aeroplanes.

Schoolchildren with outstanding fines are regularly jailed in an adult prison for nonpayment once they turn 17.

Students are also regularly fined for "disorderly behaviour", which includes playground scraps not serious enough to warrant an assault charge or for swearing or an offensive gesture. One teenage student was arrested and sent to court in Houston after he and his girlfriend poured milk on each other after they broke up. Nearly one-third of tickets involve drugs or alcohol. Although a relatively high number of tickets—up to 20% in some school districts—involve charges over the use of weapons, mostly the weapons used were fists.

The very young are not spared. According to Appleseed, Texas records show more than 1,000 tickets were issued to primary schoolchildren over the past six years (although these have no legal force at that age). Appleseed said that "several districts ticketed a six-year-old at least once in the last five years".

Fines run up to $500. For poorer parents, the cost can be crippling. Some parents and students ignore the financial penalty, but that can have consequences years down the road. Schoolchildren with outstanding fines are regularly jailed in an adult prison for nonpayment once they turn 17. Stumping up the fine is not an end to the offending student's problems either. A Class C misdemeanour is a criminal offence.

"Once you pay it, that's a guilty plea and that's on your record," said Simpkins. "In the US we have these astronomical college and university expenses and you go to fill out the ap-

School Violence in the United States

In a 2009 nationally representative sample of youth in grades 9–12:

- **11.1%** reported being in a physical fight on school property in the 12 months preceding the survey.

- **15.1%** of male students and **6.7%** of female students reported being in a physical fight on school property in the 12 months preceding the survey.

- **5.0%** did not go to school on one or more days in the 30 days preceding the survey because they felt unsafe at school or on their way to or from school.

- **5.6%** reported carrying a weapon (gun, knife or club) on school property on one or more days in the 30 days preceding the survey.

- **7.7%** reported being threatened or injured with a weapon on school property one or more times in the 12 months preceding the survey.

TAKEN FROM: "Facts at a Glance: Youth Violence 2010," Centers for Disease Control and Prevention, 2010.

plication to get your federal aid for that and it says have you ever been arrested. And there you are, no aid."

In Austin, about 3% of the school district's 80,000 pupils were given criminal citations in the 2007/8 school year, the last date for which figures are available. But the chances of a teenager receiving a ticket in any given year are much higher than that because citations are generally issued to high school pupils, not those in kindergarten or primary school.

The result, says the Appleseed report, is that "school-to-prison pipeline" in which a high proportion of children who receive tickets and end up in front of a court are arrested time and again because they are then marked out as troublemakers or find their future blighted by a criminal record.

A Judge's Experience

From her perch on the bench in an Austin courtroom, Judge Jeanne Meurer has spent close to 30 years dealing with children hauled up for infractions, some serious, others minor. Some of the difficulties faced by teachers can be seen as Meurer decides whether a parade of children should be released to await trial or held in custody. Meurer switches between motherly and intimidating depending on what she makes of the child before her.

"Some of them are rough kids," she said. "I've been on the bench 30 years and you used to never have a child cuss you out like you do now. I appreciate the frustrations that adults have in dealing with children who seem to have no manners or respect. But these are our future. Shouldn't we find a tool to change that dynamic versus just arresting them in school and coming down with the hard criminal justice hammer?"

Many of those who appear in front of Meurer have learning problems. Children with disabilities are particularly vulnerable to the consequences of police in schools. Simpkins describes the case of a boy with attention-deficit disorder who as a 12-year-old tipped a desk over in class in a rage. He was charged with threatening behaviour and sent to a juvenile prison where he was required to earn his release by meeting certain educational and behavioural standards.

Austin's school police department is well armed with officers carrying guns and pepper spray, and with dog units on call for sniffing out drugs and explosives.

"But he can't," she said. "Because of that he is turning 18 within the juvenile justice system for something that happened when he was 12. It's a real trap. A lot of these kids do have disabilities and that's how they end up there and can't get out. Instead of dealing with it within the school system like we used to, we have these school police, they come in and it escalates from there."

Sometimes that escalation involves force. "We had one young man with an IQ well below 70 who was pepper-sprayed in the hallway because he didn't understand what the police were saying," said Simpkins. "After they pepper-sprayed him he started swinging his arms around in pain and he hit one of the police officers—it's on video, his eyes were shut—and they charged him with assault of a public servant. He was 16. He was charged with two counts of assault of a public servant and he is still awaiting trial. He could end up in prison."

The Questionable Use of Force

Austin's school police department is well armed with officers carrying guns and pepper spray, and with dog units on call for sniffing out drugs and explosives.

According to the department's records, officers used force in schools more than 400 times in the five years to 2008, including incidents in which pepper spray was fired to break up a food fight in a canteen and guns were drawn on lippy students.

In recent months the questionable use of force has included the Tasering of a 16-year-old boy at a high school in Seguin, Texas, after "he refused to cooperate" when asked why he wasn't wearing his school identification tag. He then used "abusive language". The police said that when an officer tried to arrest the boy, he attempted to bite the policeman. The youth was charged with resisting arrest and criminal trespass even though the school acknowledges he is a student and was legitimately on the grounds.

Such cases are not limited to Texas. In one notorious instance in California, a school security officer broke the arm of a girl he was arresting for failing to clear up crumbs after dropping cake in the school canteen. In another incident, University of Florida campus police Tasered a student for pressing Senator John Kerry with an awkward question at a debate after he had been told to shut up.

Sometimes the force is deadly. Last week [in January 2012], Texas police were accused of overreacting in shooting dead a 15-year-old student, Jaime Gonzalez, at a school in Brownsville after he pointed an air gun, which resembled a real pistol, at them outside the principal's office. The boy's father, also called Jaime, said the police were too quick to shoot to kill when they could have wounded him or used another means to arrest him. "If they would have Tased him all this wouldn't have happened," he told the *Brownsville Herald*. "Like people say there's been standoffs with people that have hostages for hours. . . . But here, they didn't even give I don't think five minutes. No negotiating." The police say Gonzalez defied orders to put the gun down.

Meurer says she is not against police in schools but questions whether officers should regard patrolling the playground the same way they go about addressing crime on the streets.

"When you start going overboard and using laws to control non-illegal behaviour—I mean if any adult did it it's not going to be a violation—that's where we start seeing a problem," she says. "You've gradually seen this morphing from schools taking care of their own environments to the police and security personnel, and all of a sudden it just became more and more that we were relying on law enforcement to control everyday behaviour."

A Defense of the System

Chief Brian Allen, head of the school police department for the Aldine district and president of the Texas School [District] Police Chiefs' Association, is having none of it.

"There's quite a substantial number of students that break the law. In Texas and in the US, if you're issued a ticket, it's not automatically that you're found guilty. You have an opportunity to go before the judge and plead your case. If you're a teacher and a kid that's twice as big as you comes up and hits you right in the face, what are you going to do? Are you going to use your skills that they taught you or are you going to call a police officer?"

But Allen concedes that the vast majority of incidents in which the police become involved are for offences that are regarded as little more than misbehaviour elsewhere.

"Just like anything else, sometimes mistakes are made," he said. "Each circumstance is different and there's no set guideline. There's also something called officer discretion. If you take five auto mechanics and ask them to diagnose the problem of a vehicle, you'll come up with five different solutions. If you ask five different doctors to diagnose a patient, a lot of times you'll have five different diagnoses. Conversely, if you ask five different police officers if they would write a ticket or not for the same offence, you possibly have five different answers."

A Crisis of Responsibility

Parents who have been sucked into the system, such as Jennifer Rambo, the mother of Sarah Bustamantes, wonder what happened to teachers taking responsibility for school discipline.

"I was very upset at the teacher because the teacher could have just stopped it. She could have said: OK class, that's enough. She could have asked Sarah for her perfume and told her that's inappropriate, don't do that in class. But she did none of that. She called the police," she says.

Politicians and civil liberties groups have raised the same question, asking if schools are not using the police to shift responsibility, and accountability, for discipline.

"Teachers rely on the police to enforce discipline," says Simpkins. "Part of it is that they're not accountable. They're not going to get into trouble for it. The parent can't come in and yell at them. They say: It's not us, it's the police."

That view is not shared by an Austin teacher who declined to be named because he said he did not want to stigmatise the children in his class.

"There's this illusion that it's just a few kids acting up; kids being kids. This is not the 50s. Too many parents today don't control their children. Their fathers aren't around. They're in gangs. They come in to the classroom and they have no respect, no self-discipline. They're doing badly, they don't want to learn, they just want to disrupt. They can be very threatening," he says. "The police get called because that way the teacher can go on with teaching instead of wasting half the class dealing with one child, and it sends a message to the other kids."

A Necessary Policy

The Texas State Teachers Association, the state's main teachers union, did not take a position on ticketing at the recent debate in the legislature over Whitmire's proposal to scrap it. But the association's Clay Robison says that most teachers welcome the presence of police in schools.

"Obviously it looks as if some police officers are overreacting at some schools. I'm a parent and I wouldn't want my 17-year-old son hauled in to court if he and another student got into an argument in a cafeteria. Police officers need to exercise a little bit of common sense but the police are what they are. They enforce the law," he says. "At the same time, years ago, at a school in one of the better neighbourhoods of Austin, a teacher was shot to death in his classroom. It's still a very rare occurrence but it does happen. Anything that increases the security of the teacher is good so they don't have to worry about personal safety and they can concentrate on teaching the kids. We get complaints from some teachers that the police aren't aggressive enough at moving against some of the older juveniles, those that they feel actually do pose a danger to the teachers or the other students."

Because of Sarah Bustamantes's mental disorders, a disability rights group took up her case and after months of legal battles prosecutors dropped the charges. Ask her how she feels about police in schools after her experience and she's equivocal.

"We need police in school. In my school it can get physical and it can turn out very bad," she says. "But they should stop issuing tickets. Only for physical stuff or bullying. Not what you do in class."

Periodical and Internet Sources Bibliography

The following articles have been selected to supplement the diverse views presented in this chapter.

Ahmed Burić	"Federation Fails to Curb Rising Bosnian Youth Crime," *Balkan Insight*, November 9, 2011.
Economist	"Central America: The Tormented Isthmus," April 14, 2011.
Emirates 24/7	"Juvenile Delinquency on the Rise in UAE," August 7, 2011. www.emirates247.com.
Nitasha Natu	"Juvenile Crimes Get Grislier in a Desensitized World," *Times of India*, February 27, 2012.
New York Times	"Fewer Teenagers in Lockups," September 19, 2011.
Sara Sidner and Mitra Mobasherat	"Afghan Females Imprisoned for 'Moral Crimes,' Human Rights Watch Says," CNN.com, March 28, 2012.
Michael J. Sniffen	"Youth Crime Rate Down," CBS News, February 11, 2009.
Maia Szalavitz	"Study: 1 in 3 Americans Arrested by Age 23," *Heartland* (blog), December 19, 2011. http://healthland.time.com.
Sunita Toor	"British Asian Girls, Crime and Youth Justice," *Youth Justice*, vol. 9, no. 3, December 2009.
Alexandra Topping	"Knife Crime and Gang Violence on the Rise as Councils Reduce Youth Services," *Guardian* (UK), July 29, 2011.

Risk Factors for Juvenile Crime

New Zealand's Juvenile Crime Is Caused by Multiple Risk Factors

Andrew Becroft

Andrew Becroft is Principal Youth Court Judge of New Zealand. In the following viewpoint, he maintains that new research on juvenile crime in New Zealand provides insight into the risk factors that cause young people to commit criminal offenses. Becroft argues that with this new information the government can more effectively target funds and craft policies to curb juvenile crime. The most challenging segment of youth offenders will be those experiencing multiple risk factors, which the research shows leads to more hardened and recidivist offenders.

As you read, consider the following questions:

1. What percentage of young men in New Zealand will commit at least one criminal offense, according to Becroft?
2. What percentage of young males does the author estimate are committing most of the criminal offenses in New Zealand?

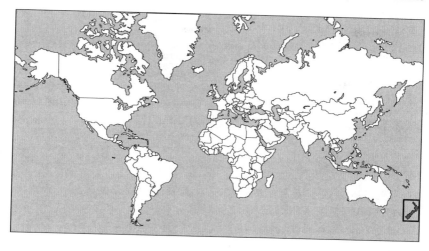

3. According to the Christchurch study, how much more likely is it that children from families with nineteen or more risk factors would end up with multiple problems as teenagers compared to children from families with six or fewer risk factors?

We are in the midst of an exciting era in New Zealand youth justice. The Children, Young Persons, and Their Families Act 1989 is twenty years old. It has proved itself as a piece of innovative legislation that has produced results in terms of reducing imprisonment and recidivism rates for children and young people. It has been studied and replicated by many international jurisdictions.

We are also seeing new research in the youth justice sector both from New Zealand and internationally. This research can help groups providing interventions for at-risk youth by giving them better, scientifically validated information, to help tie proposed interventions to the needs of offenders, and the causes of their offending. We have better information than ever before about what causes children and young people to commit crime, and how to target every dollar spent so that it produces the greatest reduction in recidivism possible.

Most importantly, the research has identified, what is obvious to those who work in this field, that "one size does not fit all". There are different types of youth offenders, and different causes of offending. These determine the type of intervention which will be effective.

Apprehension Rates for Violent Offences

Overall, apprehension rates [or arrest rates] for child and youth offending are maintaining a slow decline, with one exception. Apprehension rates for violent crime are increasing. This increase deserves special mention.

Significantly, the increase in apprehensions for violence offences amongst children and young people is replicated in all age groups. In fact the largest increase in violence crime is found in the over 50 age group! Generally, the increase in apprehension rates for violent crime for all age groups is attributed to an increase in apprehensions for domestic violence. The increased rate of apprehensions for domestic violence, in turn, is at least partly attributed to increased training by police in domestic violence.

The situation for youth, however, is somewhat different. Youth offending statistics show increases since about 2004 in both the top end (wounding with intent and injuring with intent) and bottom end (common assault and male assaults female) violent offences. These increases cannot be ignored. However, while the number of violent offences is increasing, the total numbers of young people in this age group (14 to 16 year olds) has been decreasing since 2006. It is concerning to the youth justice community that youth violence appears to be rising while the population numbers are decreasing.

Understanding the Different Types of Youth Offenders

Research shows us that around one-quarter of all young men will commit at least one offence. Of that number 80% will commit only one or two offences. The remaining 20% are responsible for 80% of New Zealand's youth offending. This pattern is as evident internationally as it is in New Zealand. It means that there is a small group (5%) of young males who are committing most offences. These are the young people who require the bulk of our attention.

Why is it that some young people commit no offences, while others commit one or two, or have extensive criminal careers? The answer is found in an analysis of the extensive research on the risk factors and protective factors for offending—that is, the environmental, social or biological factors that make a person more or less likely to commit offences.

Extensive data on risk and protective factors come from longitudinal studies, of which there are currently two in New Zealand. The Dunedin Longitudinal Study is a long-running research study of the lives of 1037 people born in Dunedin in 1972 and 1973. Study members have been assessed at regular intervals through their lives. This study has produced a large amount of information about the risk and protective factors for offending. Similarly the Christchurch Health and Development Study is following 1265 people born in the Christchurch area in the mid-1970s. These studies have revealed that youth offending tends to follow one of two types of developmental pathway.

The life-course persistent offender. The first pathway is known as the life-course persistent offender. These individuals exhibit severe behaviour problems from a very early age, sometimes as young as two years old. Their lives have been marked by multiple adverse influences including family dysfunction. As children they may have exhibited subtle cognitive deficiencies, difficult temperament or hyperactivity. When compounded by adverse environmental factors such as inadequate parenting, exposure to violence or other trauma, disrupted family bonds or poverty, their brain developmental processes responsible for social behaviour have been adversely impacted.

Life-course persistent offenders are sometimes described as having "conduct disorder". They may be aggressive, oppositional and violent. They often lack feelings of guilt, remorse, or victim empathy, and tend to be egocentric seekers of immediate gratification, who do not think about consequences. If left untreated, these behaviours escalate over the whole life span. It is apparent from the experience of the Youth Court, that 82% of this group of life-course persistent offenders are male, at least 50% are Maori [indigenous Polynesian people of New Zealand], up to 80% are not engaged with school, up to 75–80% have drug or alcohol problems. Psychological and psychiatric issues are also common.

Protective factors are positive influences in a young person's life that militate against the risk of offending . . . sometimes said to be the factors that produce resilience.

The adolescent onset offender. The second pathway is known as the adolescent onset offender. This is a much larger group (up to 80% of all youth offenders). The lives of this group of offenders are not markedly disordered, and they don't tend to exhibit disproportionate antisocial behaviour during childhood. During puberty however, behavioural issues begin to develop. The causes of their offending are due to social processes such as attachment to antisocial peers or inadequate parenting, or exposure to cannabis, rather than neurodevelopmental processes. This group is much larger in number, and unlike their life-course persistent peers, they generally experience the normal range of emotions, including remorse and willingness to put things right.

It is vitally important to keep these two categories in mind when discussing the causes and solutions to youth offending. Their differing characteristics mean that they usually demonstrate different causes of their offending, and therefore, the solutions will also be different.

"Sorry, life's cheap, but Playstations aren't!"

"Sorry, life's cheap, but Playstations aren't!," cartoon by Ian Baker. www.CartoonStock .com.

Risk and Protective Factors

A study of the causes of youth offending requires an analysis of risk and protective factors. A risk factor indicates the likelihood that a young person will commit an offence. Risk factors tend to fall into five categories—individual characteristics, family factors, school/work factors, associations with peers, and biological factors. The more risk factors a child or young person exhibits, the more likely they are to commit offences. The presence of just one risk factor is unlikely to lead to offending. The Christchurch longitudinal study found that children from families with 19 or more risk factors were 100 times more likely to end up with multiple problems as teenagers (including offending), than the 50% of the sample who had just six or fewer risk factors.

Protective factors are positive influences in a young person's life that militate against the risk of offending. Protective factors are sometimes said to be the factors that produce resilience.

While it is true that the presence of multiple risk factors increases the likelihood of a young person committing an offence, the extent to which those risk factors can be said to cause the offending is not always a straightforward relationship. Some risk factors, such as poor relationships with parents, are more direct causes of offending. Other risk factors, such as poverty or conflict between parents, have a more indirect or distal relationship to offending.

An understanding of the risk factors will provide a more structured way of identifying which young people end up offending.

It is very difficult to know which risks are actually causes, and of course, this may differ between individuals. It may be possible to look at a particular individual who has already committed an offence and determine the causes of his or her offending. But at a population level, the best information we can produce is a study of risk factors for offending, and an understanding that the more risk factors an individual possesses, the more likely they are to commit offences.

There is no single factor that can be specified as the "cause" of antisocial or criminal behaviour. The tangled roots of delinquency can, more accurately, be found in the way multiple risk factors cluster together and interact in the lives of some children, while important protective factors are conspicuously absent.

For community groups working with at-risk young people, this information is particularly relevant. An understanding of the risk factors will provide a more structured way of identifying which young people end up offending. . . .

Finding Solutions

It is impossible to be definitive about the causes of youth offending. Youth crime is not caused by a specific, easily identifiable list of factors, but by the presence in a young person's life of multiple risk factors, and the absence of protective factors. Different individuals respond to those risk and protective factors in different ways.

Instead of discussing the causes of youth offending, it is better to approach the issue by identifying the various risk factors for offending, and talk about the interventions that can either reduce those risks or increase protective factors in a young person's life.

It is also helpful in any discussion on the causes of offending to understand the two main types of offender. Life-course persistent and adolescent onset offenders have different offending profiles and differ in their background risks for offending.

Interventions with life-course persistent offenders must emphasise remedial social skills if they are to have any chance of reducing future offending and deal with conduct disorder issues. Interventions with adolescent onset offenders must address, wherever relevant, any drug and alcohol problems, anti-social peers, and parenting problems.

The Dutch Failure to Integrate Immigrant Groups Has Led to an Increase in Juvenile Crime

Soeren Kern

Soeren Kern is senior analyst for transatlantic relations at the Strategic Studies Group. In the following viewpoint, he claims that the Netherlands has a serious problem with juvenile crime committed by immigrant groups, especially the Moroccan Muslims who have settled in major cities like Amsterdam and Rotterdam. Kern lays the blame for this at the feet of Moroccan parents, who have instilled a hatred for Dutch society; left-wing intellectuals, who defend intolerance and multiculturalism; and the Dutch government, which has allowed Muslim immigrants to avoid true and effective integration in favor of failed multiculturalism. He praises recent efforts to push integrationist policies and take a tougher approach on juvenile crime committed by immigrant youth.

As you read, consider the following questions:

1. What does the author say that the crime rate is in Dutch neighborhoods where the majority of residents are Moroccan immigrants?

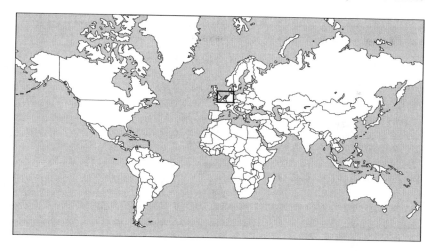

2. What is the level of Moroccan youth unemployment in the Netherlands, according to Fleur Jurgens?

3. How many Dutch Moroccans live in the Netherlands, according to the author?

Forty percent of Moroccan immigrants in the Netherlands between the ages of 12 and 24 have been arrested, fined, charged or otherwise accused of committing a crime during the past five years, according to a new report commissioned by the Dutch ministry of interior.

In Dutch neighborhoods where the majority of residents are Moroccan immigrants, the youth crime rate reaches 50%. Moreover, juvenile delinquency among Moroccans is not limited to males; girls and young women are increasingly involved in criminal activities.

The "Dutch-Moroccan Monitor 2011" ["Marokkaanse Nederlanders 2011"] also reveals that most of the Moroccan youth involved in criminal activities were born in Holland. This implies that the children of Moroccan immigrants are not integrating into Dutch society, and confirms that the Netherlands is paying dearly for its failed multicultural approach to immigration.

The report, which was produced by the Rotterdam Institute for Social Policy Research (Risbo) at the Erasmus University Rotterdam, examines the extent and nature of crime among the Dutch Moroccan population in 22 municipalities in the Netherlands. The data were taken from the Herkenningsdienstsysteem (HKS), a nationwide database where the Dutch police register criminal suspects.

Who Is to Blame?

So who is to blame for the failure of Moroccans to integrate into Dutch society and the attendant epidemic of Moroccan youth criminality?

According to Dutch journalist Fleur Jurgens in her book *The Moroccan Drama* (*Het Marokkanendrama*), the blame lies with two groups: the Moroccans, who say the Dutch are responsible for their circumstances, and left-wing multiculturalists, who have portrayed Moroccans as the defenseless victims of an unfair society.

Jurgens convincingly demolishes four multicultural myths that have been built up over the years, and which have prevented the implementation of lasting solutions.

The first myth is that there is no Moroccan problem. Jurgens answers this myth with the following statistics: over 60% of Moroccan youths between 17 and 23 drop out of school without even a basic qualification; Moroccan youth unemployment in the Netherlands is around 40%; more than 60% of Moroccan males between ages 40 and 64 live on Dutch social welfare benefits.

The second myth is that Moroccans turn to crime because the Dutch labor market discriminates against them. Jurgens refutes this by pointing out that immigrants from many countries are working in the Netherlands.

The third myth is that Moroccan parents cannot control the conduct of their sons because it is not part of their culture. Jurgens disproves this claim by showing that many Moroccan girls complain about the intense social control they face from their parents.

The fourth myth is that the Netherlands has a moral debt to the Moroccan immigrants because they were recruited as "guest workers" by the Dutch in Morocco. Jurgens refutes this argument by showing that not only was such recruitment stopped in 1973, but that at least half of the Moroccans who were recruited as guest workers eventually returned to Morocco. The present population is almost entirely made up of Moroccans who immigrated to the Netherlands on their own initiative for economic reasons.

The Dutch government now says it will abandon the long-standing model of multiculturalism that has encouraged Moroccans and other Muslim immigrants to create a parallel society within the Netherlands.

Working with Families to Tackle Youth Criminality

In January 2009, the Dutch central government signed an agreement with 22 so-called "Moroccan municipalities," home to the highest numbers of Moroccan juvenile delinquents. Over the past four years, these 22 municipalities received €32 million ($43 million) through a government program called "Moroccan Youth at Risk." Far from reducing delinquency, however, the crime rates in many of these municipalities have increased.

In most cases, the municipalities failed to implement plans for tackling youth criminality in their areas because local politicians feared reprisals from Moroccans.

The government also hired so-called "family coaches" whose job it was to interact with families with delinquent children, as well as "street coaches" who were to counsel youth on the street.

As it turned out, these trainers were more committed to preserving multiculturalism than preventing crime; many of the coaches dedicated their time to helping Moroccan youth find ways to avoid paying the fines and penalties incurred by their criminal behavior.

Jurgens concludes that Moroccan parents are to blame for the antisocial behavior of their children by teaching them at a young age to hate the Dutch and abhor their society.

Dutch politician Geert Wilders has taken Jurgens's analysis one step further by arguing that Moroccans are not integrating because they do not want to. He has told parliament that Moroccans are in the Netherlands not to integrate but rather to "subjugate the Dutch and to rule over them." He said: "They happily accept our dole, houses and doctors, but not our rules and values."

The Dutch government now says it will abandon the long-standing model of multiculturalism that has encouraged Moroccans and other Muslim immigrants to create a parallel society within the Netherlands.

The Netherlands is home to around 350,000 so-called Dutch Moroccans (Moroccan immigrants to Holland and their descendants), or around 2% of the total Dutch population of 16.4 million. More than half of Dutch Moroccans are second generation.

Mapping Out Dutch Moroccan Crime

The Dutch municipality with the highest incidence of Moroccan juvenile delinquency is the southern city of Den Bosch, where Moroccans make up approximately 10% of the total population, and where 47.7% of Moroccan males under the age of 24 have had a run-in with the law during the past five years.

Den Bosch is followed by the city of Zeist in central Netherlands (47.3%), Gouda (46.3%), Veenendaal (44.9%) and Amersfoort (44.6%). The numbers for the municipalities of

The History of Dutch Tolerance to Immigrants

The Netherlands has long had a reputation as a humanitarian haven. Famously welcoming to the Huguenots, religious and political refugees fleeing France in the 17th century, this seafaring nation has always been open when called upon to protect. Since the 16th century, refugees and immigrants have been attracted to its shores because of its tolerance and prosperity. During World War I, up to 900,000 Belgians fled to the neutral Netherlands, and 300,000 were still in the Netherlands at the end of that conflict. Almost all returned.

In the 1930s, many Jews fled from Germany and Austria to the Netherlands, as did other political refugees. By 1940 there were about 20,000 refugees from those two countries in the Netherlands. Under occupation, and with no place to hide, these refugees had to either move on or perish during the war. Most of them perished.

Following World War II, immigration resulting from the Dutch colonial heritage started. There were Dutch returnees along with the descendants of those Dutch citizens who had lived and worked in Indonesia, Suriname, and the Caribbean.

Joanne van Selm, "The Netherlands: Death of a Filmmaker Shakes a Nation," Migration Information Source, October 2005. www.migrationinformation.org.

Den Haag [The Hague], Ede, Leiden, Maassluis, Nijmegen, Oosterhout, Schiedam and Utrecht are also over 40%.

The study also reveals that Moroccan youth are substantially overrepresented (compared to other immigrant groups, such as Antilleans or Turks, or native Dutch) in every stage of the Dutch criminal justice system. In the Netherlands as a whole, Moroccan youth are overrepresented by 196%. In Den

Haag, the overrepresentation rate is 150%; in Amsterdam it is 142% and in Rotterdam it is 135%.

In nine of the 22 municipalities, however, the overrepresentation is greater than 300%. In Ede, a town in the center of the Netherlands, the overrepresentation is 481%; in Den Bosch it is 372%, in Veenendaal it is 368% and in Zeist it is 356%.

This data complements the conclusions of a classified report, "Analysis of Moroccan Criminal Populations of Municipalities in the Netherlands," conducted by the Dutch national police (KLPD) in 2009, and leaked to the media in March 2010. The report examines 14,462 Moroccan criminals in 181 Dutch municipalities.

It reveals that in absolute numbers, Amsterdam has the most Moroccan criminals (2,497), followed by Rotterdam (1,798) and Den Haag (1,271). When taking into account recidivism, the western Dutch city of Gouda has the biggest Moroccan crime problem, followed by Utrecht and Den Haag.

The report also shows the percentage of Moroccans among the total number of arrested criminals: Gouda leads with 31%, followed by Utrecht (23.7%) and Culemborg (22.6%).

Taken together, all of this data shows that efforts by the Dutch government to tackle Moroccan youth criminality have failed.

The Immigrant-Crime Connection

A separate study makes a direct link between criminality in the Netherlands and Muslim immigration. Entitled "Criminality, Migration and Ethnicity," it was published in June 2010 by the Amsterdam-based *Journal of Criminology*.

The authors of the study identified everyone who was born in the Netherlands since 1984 and tracked their criminal records until age 22. They found that in the Netherlands as a whole, 50% of Moroccan males committed a crime before they turned 22, and that one in three are repeat offenders with more than five incidents on their police records; this compares to 23% for the native Dutch. The authors also found that Moroccan girls commit three times as many crimes as native Dutch girls.

Taken together, all of this data shows that efforts by the Dutch government to tackle Moroccan youth criminality have failed.

A new integration bill, which Dutch interior minister Piet Hein Donner presented to parliament in June [2011], reads: "The government shares the social dissatisfaction over the multicultural society model and plans to shift priority to the values of the Dutch people. In the new integration system, the values of the Dutch society play a central role. With this change, the government steps away from the model of a multicultural society."

The new integration policy will place more demands on immigrants, who will be required to learn Dutch. The government has also promised to take a tougher approach toward immigrants who ignore Dutch values or disobey Dutch law.

Is it all too little too late? Many native Dutch seem to think so.

Since 2004, when the Dutch filmmaker Theo van Gogh was assassinated by a 26-year-old Dutch Moroccan, tens of thousands of native Dutch have moved to other countries in search of a better life. During the first six months of 2011 alone, 58,000 people have left the Netherlands. According to Statistics Netherlands, the increase in emigrants is largely due to native Dutch leaving the country to settle elsewhere.

The trend is picking up steam.

Brazil's Drug Mafia Is Recruiting Impoverished Children

Jens Glüsing

Jens Glüsing is a reporter for Spiegel Online. *In the following viewpoint, he chronicles the success that Brazil's brutal drug mafia has had recruiting poor and vulnerable children to commit violence on its behalf. These children are found in favelas, or shanty towns, Glüsing asserts, and often come from broken families and impoverished circumstances. Because children are treated as minors and cannot be given harsh adult sentences under Brazilian law, the author maintains, they are attractive targets for ruthless gangsters looking for young and willing enforcers.*

As you read, consider the following questions:

1. According to the author, what is the most common cause of death among Brazilian youth?

2. How many of Rio's favelas does the author say are controlled by illegal private militias?

3. Why does Comando Vermelho (Red Commando) prefer to use children and adolescents to commit crimes?

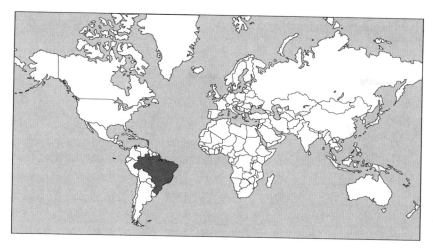

Ricardo M. was 11 years old when he killed a person for the first time. It was night, and about 20 boys had gathered at the highest point in the favela [shanty town]. With hunting rifles and assault weapons slung over their shoulders and handguns stuck into the waistbands of their Bermuda shorts, it looked as if a war were about to break out in this poverty-stricken neighborhood on the outskirts of Rio de Janeiro. After an evening spent snorting cocaine, the boys were high and completely uninhibited.

A whimpering teenager, his face disfigured from the beating he had just taken, knelt at their feet. He had been tortured with cigarettes and blades. For the boys, he was nothing but what they called an "X9"—a traitor who had informed on a gang member. The penalty was death.

The gang leader pressed a .38 caliber revolver into Ricardo's hand. Holding the heavy weapon with both hands, Ricardo held it against the offender's head and pulled the trigger. The other boys applauded and slapped Ricardo on the back. He had passed the initiation rite for membership in "Terceiro Comando," Rio's second-largest criminal organization. From then on he would be a "soldier" of the mafia. Together with the other boys, Ricardo dragged the dead boy into a ditch, poured gasoline on the body and lit a match. "I felt nothing," he says today. "I was too high."

An Epidemic of Violence

Children in Rio are waging a brutal war only a few kilometers from Brazil's famous beaches at Copacabana and Ipanema. A generation of teenagers is killing or being killed at the behest of the drug gangs that control about 300 of the city's 700 favelas. Murder is now the most common cause of death among Brazilian youth. Forty percent of all murder victims are between 15 and 25 years old.

In January [2007], for example, residents of a north Rio neighborhood found a car full of seven mutilated young bodies. The police believe they were victims of a feud between rival gangs. At least 20 young men—many of them teenagers—have died in Rio's drug wars in the last six weeks alone. Other Latin American countries face similar problems. In El Salvador, Honduras and Guatemala, adolescents are dying every day in battles between warring "maras," or youth gangs.

From Caracas to São Paulo, Mexico City to Buenos Aires, Central and South America are experiencing a dramatic upswing in youth crime. "The drug mafia recruits children as young as nine or 10," says Guaraci de Campos Viana, the chief justice of Rio de Janeiro's juvenile court. "Children have no sense of danger. Being a member of a drug gang gives them a sort of adrenaline rush."

Ricardo's Story

Ricardo began working for drug dealers when he was 10, selling small envelopes of cocaine on the street. At 11 he was promoted to the job of "radio," which involves sitting on roofs, keeping an eye out for unfamiliar faces and using a walkietalkie to report their approach. He began snorting cocaine to stay awake. His mother, a maid, lost control over her son long ago. He doesn't know who his father is.

For Ricardo, part of becoming a "soldier" meant swearing to abide by the unwritten law of the Terceiro Comando: never steal from anyone in the favela and never take away a friend's woman. His promotion came with a hefty pay increase. He was now earning 250 Real (€90) a day. While other children his age attended school, Ricardo lived the life of a favela prince. He treated himself to multiple girlfriends, bought them clothes and presents, and was respected. "My life revolved around sex, drugs and weapons," he says. Eventually he would probably have become a "gerente," or head of a drug-selling operation, if he hadn't been arrested after someone tipped off the police. Ricardo is now 17 and an inmate at the "Escola João Luiz Alves," a juvenile correctional facility. His face is covered with acne and his arms with tattoos. He remains loyal to his gang, even in prison.

The drug gangs are often so well armed that only heavily armed special units dare to enter the favelas.

Gangs, in fact, are in control of most Brazilian prisons. Last year [2006] Marcos Marcola, the leader of the PCC [Primeiro Comando da Capital] criminal gang, used a mobile phone to direct his gang's attacks on buses, banks and police stations in São Paulo—from his prison cell. More than 100 people died, and all because Marcola refused to be transferred to a high-security prison.

In December the jailed bosses of "Comando Vermelho" (Red Commando) ordered similar attacks in Rio, costing 20 people their lives. Seven were burned alive when the gangsters refused to allow their victims to get off buses to which they had set fire. Brazilian president Luiz Inácio Lula da Silva referred to the incidents as acts of "terrorism."

Fighting for Control

The drug mafia began resorting to such violence after it became a target itself. Private militias are trying to expel the

---

Rio Turns to Community Policing to Fight Drug Mafia

Members of the unit are able to draw on sound intelligence, using their physical proximity to the community to gather valuable information to better combat crime. UPP [Police Pacification Unit] police officers are highly visible, as they establish a base in the strategic heart of each favela—usually in the same place from which drug dealers formerly staged their operations.

Albert Souza Mulli,
"Patrolling Rio's Favelas—From Pacification to Police State?,"
ISN Insights, April 19, 2011. www.isn.ethz.ch.

---

drug dealers from many slums. The illegal militias, which enjoy excellent relations with the police and force residents to pay them protection money, already control 97 of Rio's favelas.

The government is almost completely absent from most slums and police presence is rare. The drug gangs are often so well armed that only heavily armed special units dare to enter the favelas. Police officers, many in the drug dealers' pay, look the other way when the gangs go to war, uninterested in endangering their own illegal earnings from the cocaine trade. Corruption reaches right to the top ranks of law enforcement. The public prosecutor's office is currently investigating Rio's former police chief for taking bribes from the mafia.

President Lula, for his part, has had enough and has now brought in the military in an attempt to tackle the problem. Lawmakers are also considering amending the law so that even 16-year-olds can be sentenced to lengthy prison terms.

Just in the last three weeks, Brazilian youth perpetrated three robberies and murders. Brazilians were particularly shocked by the death of a six-year-old boy, João Hélio Fernandes [Vieites]. His mother was attacked when she stopped her car at a street corner. When she was unable to unbuckle her son's seat belt, the attackers drove off, dragging the boy along as he hung like a puppet from the car—for seven kilometers. When the boy's body was found, his head, knees and fingers were gone. One of the attackers was only 16.

The drug mafia takes advantage of the fact that minors cannot be given adult prison sentences. Comando Vermelho prefers to use children and adolescents to commit its robberies and murders, because they have so few inhibitions. Ricardo M. describes how he sawed off the arms and legs of prisoners while they were still alive. "We had a special table that we used to torture traitors." If they are apprehended, the underage gang members spend only a few months in prison and usually return to their gangs shortly after being released.

Girls and the Drug Mafia

Girls are also involved in the drug mafia. Fabiana S., 15, an exceptionally pretty and intelligent girl, became the head of a drug-selling operation at the age of 12. Her father watches over parked cars for a pittance and her mother works as a maid. The family lives in a favela in Niterói, a Rio suburb.

Fabiana was expelled from school when she was 11. "I was too rebellious," she says. When the local head of Comando Vermelho offered her a job, she accepted. Her first job was to weigh and package cocaine into small envelopes, which are sold for the equivalent of two, four or eight euros. Her customers were workers from a nearby shipyard.

The gang leaders quickly recognized their young manager's commercial skills and gave her the job of keeping records of the bribes they paid to the police. She was soon in charge of buying drugs. At 14 Fabiana was earning the equivalent of €800 a month, a princely sum in the favelas. She bought a house and went shopping with her sister twice a week. She offered her parents money, but they refused. "My mother says there is blood on the bills," she says.

But Fabiana didn't care.

Naturally, she knew about the secret cemetery at the top of the hill, where drug dealers buried their victims. "Sometimes the bodies were exposed when it rained." Most of the dead were young girls. "Many of them would go to bed with the dealers for a pinch of cocaine," she says. "Later on they would have affairs with police officers and become traitors."

Fabiana was also fond of snorting cocaine. She was careful to remain faithful to her boyfriend, partly for her own safety. "He was a drug boss. There could have been problems." The couple would spend their evenings stealing cars at gunpoint and racing around Rio. The police pursued and arrested them during one of these joy rides.

Fabiana now plans to build a new life. "Seven of my friends were shot to death, I don't want that to happen to me," she says. She plans to go back to school, learn English and attend college. But former child gangsters have few prospects in the job market.

Ricardo M., the soldier from the Terceiro Comando gang, will also be released soon. What does he plan to do? "I'll look for a job," he says. And if he doesn't find one? Ricardo grins. "The drug dealers will always have work for me."

Palestinian Girls Turn to Crime to Escape Troubled Family Lives

Anjuli Bedi

Anjuli Bedi is a correspondent for Global Press Institute. In the following viewpoint, she reports on the disturbing trend of young Palestinian girls intentionally provoking Israeli soldiers at the Qalandia checkpoint, which is located between Jerusalem and Ramallah. Bedi found that these girls were looking to escape violent or oppressive domestic situations and viewed Israeli prison to be a preferable option to remaining at home with their families. Some Palestinian authorities have questioned the veracity of the statements of these girls, Bedi asserts, and have argued that specific charges against the girls were too harsh.

As you read, consider the following questions:

1. According to Mahmoud Malik, how many Palestinian girls in Israeli detention centers in 2009 admitted to committing crimes to escape domestic issues?

2. Why did Bara'a report that she made a threat with a knife at the Qalandia checkpoint?

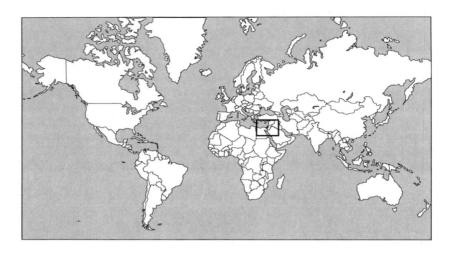

3. According to Mona Zaghrout, how many girls released from prison have come to the counseling program at the YMCA between May and September 2010, when this viewpoint was written?

Beside the separation wall near Qalandia checkpoint sits a military court, a set of portable buildings, where Palestinian citizens are tried for committing crimes against the state of Israel. In the chaotic and crowded hearing room, an 18-year-old girl sits with her feet shackled as she waits for proceedings to start.

She appears buoyant as she carries on a lively conversation with her grandfather across the room. On the surface, she seems unconcerned with her freedom. At today's hearing Aisha's attorney will attempt to reduce her 24-month sentence. The court proceedings and the circumstances of her arrest are familiar territory for the teen.

Aisha, whose last name was withheld at her attorney's request, was arrested two years earlier when, at 16, she walked to a military checkpoint in her hometown of Hebron, drew a knife, and announced that she intended to stab an Israeli soldier.

Her former attorney, Ibrahim Hamza, from Defense for Children International, DCI, says upon reviewing her case, he discovered that she dealt with significant domestic violence at home. The court psychologist confirmed his initial assessment and Aisha's sentence was reduced from 24 to 10 months. The judge warned Aisha that if she committed the same crime again, she would receive the full sentence. Now, Aisha has been arrested for committing the exact same crime—threatening to kill an Israeli soldier with a knife, at a checkpoint.

For these girls, detention centers are not always perceived as a place of imprisonment. For many, they are a preferable alternative to their situations at home.

A Shocking Trend

Many court cases dealing with young Palestinian girls arrested in the West Bank tend to follow this pattern. Mahmoud Malik, who requested his full name not be used, an advocate with DCI, reported that as many as six Palestinian girls in Israeli detention centers who were arrested in 2009 admitted to committing crimes to escape domestic issues. For these girls, detention centers are not always perceived as a place of imprisonment. For many, they are a preferable alternative to their situations at home.

Intentional arrest is a sensitive issue here that is debated by many. While attorneys and child advocates have researched the phenomenon and have collected affidavits by many girls who say they sought arrest, many others say this is just another example of Israeli officers playing politics with Palestinian youth. Still, one counselor with the YMCA in Beit Sahour says often the girls who come out of prison, after having a reprieve from their difficult family lives, have a renewed sense of strength and purpose.

DCI's 2009 annual report included an affidavit from a 14-year-old girl identified as Bara'a M., who, like Aisha, went to

Qalandia checkpoint with a knife hidden up the sleeve of her jacket. When she was asked why she had a knife, she said, "I have problems with my family and I came to the checkpoint to get arrested."

The issue of intentional arrest by teenaged Palestinians remains largely unrecognized here.

At age 7, Bara'a says she was forced to wear a hijab and two years later, her family made her wear a jilbab, a full-length coat, which caused her to feel stifled and imprisoned. "Basically, they took away my freedom," she told DCI.

Her friend, identified in the report as Samah S., also 14, accompanied her to the checkpoint and secured her own arrest by carrying a kitchen knife in her purse. She was motivated to do so for a very specific reason, writing in her affidavit, "My family wanted me to marry a 35-year-old policeman and I refused. It was supposed to take place two or three days from now. I therefore decided to head to the checkpoint and do anything that would get me arrested."

The issue of intentional arrest by teenaged Palestinians remains largely unrecognized here. But many others here do not believe the DCI report and have alternate interpretations of the arrests.

Are the Charges True?

Ayman Ramahi, former head of the education center at the Jalazone refugee camp near Ramallah, where the two girls, Bara'a and Samah, are from, says he believes the Israeli security forces at Qalandia fabricated the charges against the girls.

"Who can go there with a knife or anything else to stab a soldier at a checkpoint like Qalandia?" he said. "It's unbelievable that anyone who has a mind would try this."

He admits that in places like Hebron, domestic problems exist within homes or communities but he says life in Jalazone is different. "If you talk about somewhere like Jalazone, the girls have freedom to do what they want, they have full access to education, treatment, everything," he says, adding that his own daughter is studying at the university level.

However, despite Ramahi's allegations, the Israeli soldiers at the checkpoints have not been accused of fabricating evidence in these cases, as many of the girls admitted in their affidavits that they carried those knives to the checkpoint with a specific intention.

Harsh Treatment

Malik of DCI says that while the girls' intentions were clear, the specific charges against some of these girls are questionable. Samah S. for example was charged with the crime of "intending to kill an Israeli soldier." According to DCI, when she arrived at Qalandia checkpoint she never removed the kitchen knife from her bag, it was found by security forces who searched her. In her affidavit, she claims that during her interrogation security forces continually screamed at her, "You came here to stab a soldier!" In her affidavit, she explained to the interrogator she was attempting to get away from home, yet after intense questioning, she relented and agreed with the claim that she intended to stab a soldier.

Mona Zaghrout, head of the counseling and supervision department at the YMCA Rehabilitation Program in the town of Beit Sahour, says after these girls are released from prison they experience difficulties readjusting to daily life. Since May of 2010, Zaghrout says only three girls released from prison have come to the counseling program at the YMCA. "The girls came out of prison very nervous and having less confidence in themselves, their families and their community," she says.

But Zaghrout says she does see a positive side to time spent in prison and away from families. "The positive thing is that after working with them, they insist on challenging themselves, their families, and the community by building strong futures for themselves," she says.

The Australian Juvenile System Is Discriminatory Against Aboriginal Youth

Kathy Marks

Kathy Marks is a correspondent for the Christian Science Monitor. *In the following viewpoint, Marks discusses the deaths of several Australian Aboriginal youths who have died while incarcerated or in police custody, bringing national attention to the disproportionate number of incarcerated Aborigines in Australia. Young Aborigines are twenty-eight times more likely to end up in juvenile detention; critics say this is primarily the result of discrimination, as many youth are arrested for minor offenses. To change the system, Marks asserts, it is important to end Australia's denial of racism, which perpetuates the problem.*

As you read, consider the following questions:

1. Why, according to the viewpoint, was Mulrunji Doomadgee arrested?

2. What did the royal commission studying indigenous deaths in custody recommend in its findings?

3. What is the "justice reinvestment" approach, according to the viewpoint?

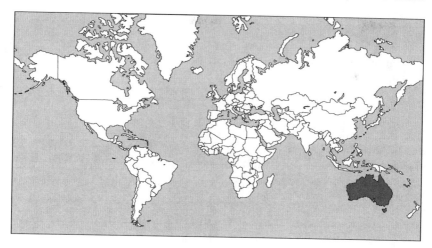

The death of several Australian Aborigines who have died in prison or police custody around the country recently [in 2010] has underscored the disproportionately high percentage of Aborigines among the country's incarcerated—a result in part of overcrowded housing and low education rates that go hand in hand with violence and petty crime. But discrimination is also to blame, say critics.

The picture is especially bleak for young indigenous people, who are 28 times more likely to end up in juvenile detention according to the latest official figures. In one notorious case last November, police charged a 12-year-old boy in Western Australia with receiving a chocolate frog allegedly stolen from a supermarket.

Aboriginal adults are six times more likely to be arrested than other Australians and 13 times more likely to be jailed. In the Northern Territory, they make up 80 percent of the prison population although only one-third of the territory's residents are indigenous.

The Case of Mulrunji Doomadgee

A young man named Mulrunji Doomadgee, of Palm Island off Queensland's coast, was one such Australian Aborigine who was caught up in the criminal justice system. Arrested for drunkenness and swearing, he was found dead in a cell after a struggle with the policeman who had brought him in, Chris Hurley.

Critics say Doomadgee's offense is precisely the type that does not warrant automatic arrest and imprisonment.

"The initial apprehension and locking up of Mulrunji Doomadgee were as much an issue as what happened afterwards," says Chris Cunneen, a law professor at the University of New South Wales. "They showed how police are far too ready to arrest and take Aboriginal people into custody in situations where there would be alternatives available."

In a 2005 inquest into Doomadgee's death, Mr. Hurley—the first officer ever charged in relation to the death of an Aborigine in custody—was found responsible for the prisoner's fatal injuries. But he was acquitted of manslaughter and continues to serve in the Queensland force. A second inquest was launched earlier this month, at the same time that relatives and supporters of another prisoner who died in state custody, Stephen Currie, were protesting at the state parliament building in Brisbane.

A royal commission studying indigenous deaths in custody found that Aboriginal people were much more likely to be incarcerated than their white counterparts.

Meanwhile, a number of Palm Islanders, who in 2004 protested Doomadgee's death, are serving jail sentences.

Alfred Lacey, the island's mayor, says that while the protesters were quickly jailed, he and his fellow Aborigines are still waiting for justice to be served in Doomadgee's case.

"The law was very quick to move on the blackfellas [Aborigines] after the rioting and make sure they got locked up," argues Mr. Lacey. "But we're still waiting for justice on the

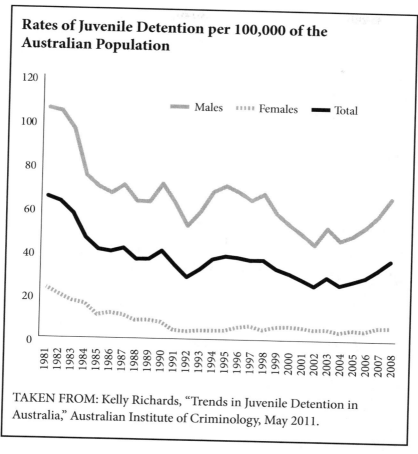

Rates of Juvenile Detention per 100,000 of the Australian Population

TAKEN FROM: Kelly Richards, "Trends in Juvenile Detention in Australia," Australian Institute of Criminology, May 2011.

other side of the fence. That's the reason why Aboriginal people in this country will never have faith in the system: It doesn't treat us equally."

Royal Commission's Recommendations Not Implemented

Two decades ago, a royal commission studying indigenous deaths in custody found that Aboriginal people were much more likely to be incarcerated than their white counterparts. Among its key recommendations were that arrests should be made only if absolutely necessary and suspects should be imprisoned only as a last resort.

Social justice campaigners say there is little sign of that advice being heeded today.

Criminologists say there are numerous reasons why indigenous Australians are detained and locked up in much higher numbers than everyone else. Over-policing is one, they say. But social and economic disadvantage also plays a major part. Aboriginal populations have elevated rates of poverty and unemployment. They live in overcrowded housing, have poorer health, and are relatively uneducated. All these factors contribute to violence and petty crime.

"Justice Reinvestment" Approach

The Australian Human Rights Commission (AHRC), an independent statutory body, wants the government to try to reduce the number of Aboriginal people in custody by diverting some public funds that would be spent on imprisonment into problem communities. The "justice reinvestment" approach is aimed at preventing young people, in particular, from offending by providing community services and programs that address the causes of crime.

In parts of the United States, this approach has been implemented with apparently strong results. According to the AHRC, there was a 72 percent drop in juvenile incarceration in Oregon after funds were reinvested in restorative justice and community service programs.

The AHRC's Aboriginal and Torres Strait Islander Social Justice Commissioner, Mick Gooda, says: "One of the biggest problems we have in this country is denial of racism. I keep saying to people: Come and live in my world for a while and you might change your opinion."

Scotland Should Be More Responsive to the Needs of At-Risk Children

Rory Cahill

Rory Cahill is a reporter for Holyrood. *In the following viewpoint, he argues that recent controversy over some proposed reforms to the Children's Hearings system highlights the urgency to be more responsive to the needs of at-risk children in Scotland. Cahill points to the issue of criminal responsibility, arguing that Scotland should raise it to be more in line with other European countries. He also underlines the need to reform the secure care system to better protect vulnerable young people.*

As you read, consider the following questions:

1. Does the author believe that the ASBO culture caught on in Scotland?
2. What is the age of criminal responsibility in Scotland?
3. What incident in September 2009 does the author think put a spotlight on the issue of secure care?

For a long time, we in Scotland have congratulated ourselves on how advanced our Children's Hearings system is. With our welfare-based approach to children and young

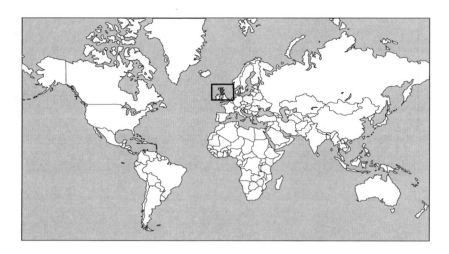

people who are coming into contact with the justice system, or who are in situations where they are being left vulnerable to abuse or neglect, we felt we had a far more nuanced and effective approach than many other nations, especially that one south of the border.

Then the arrival of [former British prime minister] Tony Blair's Respect agenda—remember that?—changed the landscape greatly. Now the talk was of yobs and antisocial behaviour orders (ASBOs) [an order that addresses behaviours such as swearing or underage drinking] and responsibilities as well as rights. The ASBO culture, despite the best efforts of former first minister Jack McConnell and his justice minister Cathy Jamieson, who was famously photographed being subjected to some rather antisocial behaviour herself, never took hold here.

A Welcome Change in Tone

The SNP [Scottish National Party, a political party] were elected on a promise of doing away with a policy which it said criminalised our young people and they did indeed remove the emphasis from ASBOs. The various groups and campaigners for children and young people's rights who had been so appalled by the Labour switch to what they saw as a more authoritarian approach were overjoyed.

"Their tone has generally been positive and I welcome that. The language that the new administration is using is one of prevention and support and early intervention, all of which are welcome and in particular, they have been receptive to talk about children's rights and been very responsive to the concluding observations of the UN [United Nations] monitoring committee on the UN Convention on the Rights of the Child and I really welcome that. It gives a good platform for the work of this office but also in terms of where we can make improvements for children and young people. So generally, I welcome the tone and the language that has been used since the new administration came to power," says Tam Baillie, the new commissioner for children and young people and a long-time campaigner in Scotland.

Unpopular Reforms

But for many—Baillie included—the SNP's honeymoon ended when it proposed major reforms to the Children's Hearings system. The draft Children's Hearing bill would have seen the creation of a new body, the Scottish Children's Hearing Tribunal, to oversee the 32 current panels and carry out training and recruitment presently run by local councils. However, the plan was met with fierce resistance, with some existing Children's Panel members threatening to resign.

One critic, Philip White, chairman of the Argyll and Bute panel, said the changes were "unwelcome, unwanted and unnecessary." The union UNISON also criticised aspects of the draft bill, claiming it focused "disproportionately" on offences, given that two-thirds of referrals to children's reporters, and 40,000 out of 50,000 hearings last year [2008], related to welfare concerns rather than offending.

Opposition parties, notably Labour, also voiced their strong opposition to the bill.

Baillie himself says he "shares the concerns that had been expressed" about it. As a result, the government says it will delay the bill to reassess its direction and focus.

For the Scottish Children's Reporter Administration, which will be heavily impacted by any changes, the pause will allow time to ensure the best possible legislation is passed.

The government has announced its intention to raise the age of criminal prosecution which will mean that for those offences which would normally have gone to an adult court, they no longer will.

Principal reporter/chief executive, Netta Maciver, says: "The Children's Hearings system has been around for some time, and like any other system can benefit from improvement. Understanding how it works and how it could work better is part of the challenge now, as we move towards the introduction of a bill early in 2010. We will want to retain the best of what is there, and improve any area that will increase the benefits for children, their families and the communities they live in." A revised bill will inevitably emerge and will most likely pass through Parliament in some form. But this does not mean that the world of youth justice in Scotland no longer requires reform. In fact, Baillie argues that it should signal the beginning of even greater change.

"I share the view that we do need to update and bring the hearings into line with the other legislative requirements, particularly [the] European Convention on Human Rights. There is a need to look at processes in the hearing system. Beyond that, though, I think we should be looking at how responsive the hearing system is to the needs and ultimately the rights of children.

"However, it is not perfect and it never has been perfect. For instance, at age eight, we have one of the lowest ages of criminal responsibility in Europe and we are regularly criticised by the UN committee and I think we should do some-

The Neglect of Scottish Criminology

It is argued that issues of crime and criminal justice in Scotland (as is the case for Northern Ireland and Wales) have been generally neglected in British criminology. A 'tartan' lens, or gaze, reveals that all too often 'British' means 'English', exemplified in the 'British Crime Survey', although it should be noted that more comparative figures are now available, albeit 'English' centred. It is also seen in major texts, and in the discourse of theoretical discussions of, for example, youth gangs or race, ethnicity, crime and criminal justice. Valuable opportunities for comparative research are thereby missed.

Hazel Croall, "Criminal Justice, Social Inequalities and Social Justice in Scotland," OpenLearn LabSpace, February 10, 2011. http://labspace.open.ac.uk.

thing about that. We shouldn't be describing our eight-year-olds as young offenders. The government has announced its intention to raise the age of criminal prosecution which will mean that for those offences which would normally have gone to an adult court, they no longer will. But there is still an issue about the age of criminal responsibility.

"We have got a welfare-based hearing system for our children under 16 and for those who are under supervision at age 16 but we still have got very high numbers of children aged 16 and 17 held in young offenders' institutions and that brings into question the overall juvenile justice system, as to why we lock up so many of our 16- and 17-year-olds," he says.

The Issue of Secure Care

Then there is the issue of secure care.

No discussion about our care system can now be had without reference to the tragic deaths of Neve Lafferty, 15, and her friend Georgia Rowe, 14, who jumped off the Erskine Bridge last month [September 2009]. Neither girl was in secure care at the Good Shepherd Centre in Bridgeton, leading to calls for security to be improved at such facilities to prevent vulnerable youngsters from taking similar steps.

But conversely, at the same time, the SNP is overseeing a reduction in the number of secure care beds—which are very expensive.

Baillie says it is vital to look at the issue in the round and not allow the emotional impact of one case to colour a debate that will have long-term implications for the country.

He says: "There are a number of forces at play here. The increase in the bed spaces was as a result of pressure on the bed spaces, the number of secure places we had. The increases came under another administration. At the same time, you had very much increased resources put into supporting children in the community. That was actually on the back of ASBO legislation but nonetheless we have got increased resources in terms of that particular group and councils have now got some leeway in putting additional resources into children who may otherwise have been received into secure care.

"And of course you do have very tight budgets for councils. They are under a great deal of pressure to look at alternatives in terms of the costs. All of those have led, I think, it's difficult to quantify, but I think all of those factors play a part leading to very costly empty bed spaces with the secure estate."

The Caribbean Youth Crime Rate Is Affected by the Region's Social and Economic Problems

Jeevan Robinson

Jeevan Robinson is editor in chief of MNI Alive. In the following viewpoint, he assesses the epidemic of youth crime that has swept through the Caribbean, much of it spurred by the widespread availability of guns. Robinson speculates that this rise in juvenile crime is caused by the intensification of social ills, particularly the global economic crisis and deepening poverty; the crumbling of communities; an abandonment of organized religion; and a cultural emphasis on materialism. He also points to the lack of opportunities—academically, creatively, and economically—in the region for energetic and ambitious young people.

As you read, consider the following questions:

1. According to a UN Office on Drugs and Crime (UNODC) report, what percentage of all murder committed within the Caribbean and Central America are inflicted by guns?

2. What was the murder rate in St. Kitts and Nevis in 2010, according to the UNODC report?

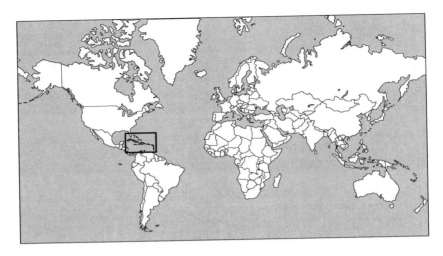

3. What does Robinson say is the role of the Youth Gangs and Violence consultations?

When [Jamaican athlete] Usain Bolt breaks world records and strikes his famous victory pose, Caribbean people are united with pride. When the West Indies cricket team suckers a rare victory, Caribbean people become united with optimism. But when the United Nations Office on Drugs and Crime (UNODC) report that Caribbean young men are second only to those in Central America to be killed by guns, I am undecided if we should collectively hang our heads in shame or be stricken with bewilderment. Both?

The Role of Guns

A report being circulated by the aforementioned UNODC, looking at crime levels around the world has singled out the Caribbean and Central America for having 'near crisis point' levels of murders. The report mentions that 3/4 of all murders committed within these two regions are inflicted by guns. An increase in firearms usage is seen as the main cause for the increase in the Caribbean's murder rate.

These statistics by the UNODC on crime levels in the Caribbean did not shock me frankly. I am concerned, though, to know what is causing the increase and what are the effects of the rising levels of youth crime on the region. I stated that the statistics did not shock me because there are several Caribbean territories that, for some time now, have been reporting rising levels of crime. Persons cannot now continue to berate Jamaica about its annual murder rate, when other islands, particularly the smaller ones, have been escalating their very own crime numbers. It has become a region-wide pandemic that requires creative and definitive measures to nip it in the bud.

Acts of crime in their various manifestations are in effect social ills.

To paint a clearer picture, the statistics as released from the UNODC study are as follows:

- 1,428 people were murdered in Jamaica in 2010, with firearms accounting for 52.1%

- St. Kitts and Nevis had a murder rate of 38.2%

- The United States Virgin Islands at 39.1%

- Trinidad and Tobago 35.2%

- Guyana 18.4%

- Barbados 11.3%

- Cuba 4.6%

- Anguilla, Antigua and Barbuda both at 6.8%

- British Virgin Islands at 8.6%

- Belize 41.7%

But what is the cause of these rising crime levels and why are we seeing crime rates amongst young men, specifically, skyrocketing in the region? Some would propose that it is mainly due to an increase in the illicit drugs trade throughout the region that causes gun violence and gang culture to prolif-

The Key Role of School Attendance in Fighting Juvenile Crime

Recent empirical research conducted on risk and protective factors for youth in the Caribbean concluded that school attendance/connectedness are the most important factors in reducing violent youth behavior. In particular, the study found that boys (girls) who feel connected to school were 60 percent (55 percent) less likely to engage in violent activity. In addition, the study showed the significant effects that schools have in reducing drug use, smoking, and alcohol consumption. The study also found that family connectedness, or the presence of a caring adult, served as the second most important protective factor. The analysis concluded that both risk and protective factors are cumulative; if protective influences are held constant and predominant risks are added one at a time, risk behavior rises significantly. Conversely, and perhaps more importantly, when risk factors are held constant and protective factors are added, there is an even greater reduction in reported involvement with violence.

"Crime, Violence, and Development:
Trends, Costs, and Policy Options in the Caribbean,"
World Bank and United Nations Office
on Drugs and Crime (UNODC), March 2007.

erate. I am not certain I am sold on this as the 'main' reason. Without a doubt, it is a contributing factor, as the UNODC study concludes, "In Central America and the Caribbean, changes in drug trafficking markets have, in one way or another, contributed to rising levels of homicide."

The Cause of Youth Crime

Acts of crime in their various manifestations are in effect social ills. There are several possible occurrences that can be attributed as very plausible conditions for this upsurge in crime in the Caribbean. I am considering several areas: Are we seeing a direct rise in the social ills of the Caribbean and a resultant inflation of our crime numbers, based on increased poverty in the affected islands? The global economic crisis will most surely be harshly felt in developing nations with limited resources, such as the Caribbean islands. Another point that comes to mind is are we standing as spectators to the crumbling of our communities and value structures, [while] the youths are carefree in their crime spree? Communities may have become so dismantled that respect is alien, materialism is king and the church is a chore attended only to appease, but less so for moral and ethical grounding?

And lastly, has the political directorate in some of these islands failed the youths in providing adequate avenues for them to express themselves creatively, academically and socially? When our young children leave school in the islands, for those that cannot go to university or relocate abroad to the diaspora, what are the avenues that present themselves that they feel they too can be empowered to earn a decent living and improve their quality of life? These are serious questions that require individual probing as real contributing factors that may be pushing our young men towards gangs, drugs and murder.

Just last month [September 2011] Sam Condor, deputy prime minister and foreign minister of St. Kitts and Nevis, addressed the United Nations. What I noted most from Condor's presentation was his position that the surge in violence in the Caribbean was also symptomatic of deeper community and social issues in the countries of the region. That statement from Condor spoke directly to the root of the problem, which to me shows that he understands that attacking the problem from its incubation stages is crucial towards making any progress towards curbing the worrying upward trend in youth crime and murder.

Positive Developments

There are though positive developments now taking place to redress this rise in murder and youth crime in the Caribbean. The CARICOM [Caribbean Community] Secretariat, in collaboration with the United Nations Development Programme (UNDP), has organized a series of subregional consultations called Youth Gangs and Violence: Partnering for Prevention and Social Development. These consultations will be looking to discuss antigang programmes and services as part of a wider action plan. This first aspect of the action plan will look to provide support services, from the community level, to reduce involvement in gang life and to equip 'gang leavers' with life skills to help them reintegrate into normal society.

Reclaiming the high ground would be paramount for many of these islands that have seen an escalation in murder and crime. In our developing states, criminals cannot be seen to run riot and to be inducing fear in communities. Such scenarios would stand contrary to what a progressive nation should be seeking to encourage.

Periodical and Internet Sources Bibliography

The following articles have been selected to supplement the diverse views presented in this chapter.

Joel D. Adriano	"Wasted Youth in the Philippines," *Asia Times Online*, October 15, 2011. www.atimes.com.
David Blanchflower	"As the Jobs Continue to Go, the Crime Wave Will Grow," *New Statesman*, July 8, 2011.
Alexander Busansky	"Research as Poverty Fighter: The Link Between Poverty, Child Welfare, and Criminal Justice," Spotlight on Poverty and Opportunity, May 31, 2011. www.spotlightonpoverty.org.
Rory Carroll	"Honduras: 'We Are Burying Kids All the Time,'" *Guardian* (UK), November 12, 2010.
Erik Eckholm	"Gang Violence Grows on an Indian Reservation," *New York Times*, December 13, 2009.
Pallavi Gupta	"Juvenile Delinquency and Rising Crimes," Youth Ki Awaaz, April 2012. www.youthkiawaaz.com.
Shalom Hammer	"The Ramifications of Freedom," *Jerusalem Post*, March 28, 2012.
Paul Letiwa	"Kenya: Youth and Crime: Blame It All on Absentee Parents and Poverty," *Daily Nation* (Kenya), August 1, 2011.
Shira Poliak	"Child Poverty Rates Increase Among Immigrants," *Jerusalem Post*, July 14, 2011.
Alan White	"The Issues Surrounding Youth Crime," *New Statesman*, April 23, 2012.

GLOBALVIEWPOINTS

CHAPTER 3

Debates over the Juvenile Justice System

Tanzanian Juvenile Institutions May Be Doing More Harm than Good

Sharifa Kalokola

Sharifa Kalokola is a reporter for the Citizen. *In the following viewpoint, she scrutinizes the juvenile detention centers in Tanzania and finds that many authorities believe they are necessary as a last resort for juvenile delinquents in today's society. Kalokola reports that the rise in juvenile crime is due to parental neglect and a tough economic situation. There is a general consensus, asserts Kalokola, that Tanzanian authorities have a lot of work to do reforming and upgrading the country's juvenile justice system to meet the needs of troubled youths and to meet international human rights standards.*

As you read, consider the following questions:

1. According to Kalokola, what is the range of the children at the detention center in Upanga, Dar es Salaam?

2. How did the Sexual Offences Special Provisions Act of Tanzania change the minimum age of criminal responsibility in 1998?

3. According to assessments, what is the most frequent crime committed by juveniles in Tanzania?

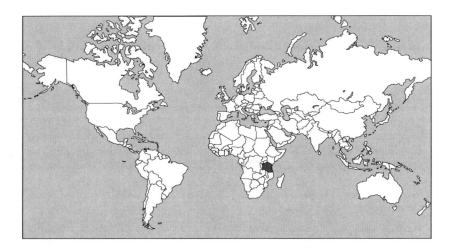

On the outside, it looks like a perfect school, with a welcoming atmosphere. But the tightly locked gates and tight security are too unsettling to keep visitors under the illusion of entering a normal academic centre. Yet like a serious learning institution, behind the fence, all is quiet and clean. And cleared by security at the gate, walking past the entrance, it does not suddenly dawn on the visitor that this is a correctional facility.

In fact, entering a nearby dormitory one gets the feeling that some pieces of old furniture showing off years of neglect are a misfit in this otherwise peaceful place. There are beds with no mattresses that seem not to belong here.

The walls of the dormitory add to the feeling that this is a rare academic institution. The colourful and expressive artwork of children playing and reading are comforting and gives the place a homely atmosphere.

It is exactly what one sees in kindergarten schools.

But a few more minutes of going through a set of strict rules at one corner of the dormitory leave you with no illusions of where you have found yourself in. More so, it gives you a real glimpse of the kind of life teenagers holed up at the juvenile correctional institution in Upanga, Dar es Salaam, lead.

The institution, with capacity to hold up to 60 people, was established 49 years ago, and it is where children accused of committing various crimes in Dar es Salaam and the Coast regions are remanded to a correctional programme.

How effective this programme is or has been is better left for teenagers like Zaituni, 13, one of the children at the centre, to bear witness.

A Blessing in Disguise

Getting access to talk to Zaituni and her colleagues is tough because of privacy issues with security, but when I finally did, I find her in a classroom. Her teacher sitting down beside her, she is writing as the instructor explains something.

"To me this has been a blessing in disguise because I have benefitted from my stay at the centre," says the 13-year-old girl.

At an orphanage where she used to stay before coming to the juvenile institution, Zaituni was accused of stealing two mobile phones from her neighbours. That is how she found herself at the correctional facility, where she has learnt how to read and write.

"But when I came here, I thought it was all about punishment. It was a real pleasure to realise there are some things I could learn from here—I can now write my name," says the teenager from Arusha, who had not been inside a classroom before.

The ages of children at the centre range from 10 to 18. There are two social welfare officers, two teachers, three matrons and three security guards, three cooks and one driver, to take care of the teenagers, according to Alex Bwire, the officer in charge of the institution.

"Many children come here full of anguish and with an attitude. But we know how to handle them," says officer Bwire, a tough-talking man, whose good humour betrays a softer nature that is alien to people in his position.

Forced to Use Corporal Punishment

He adds: "We are sometimes forced to use corporal punishment to make the children behave. It can take a long time before they calm down, especially drug addicts. But we help them to accept their situation and to understand that they are here to learn to be good citizens."

The juvenile justice system has evolved over the years based on the premise that juveniles are different from adults and that juveniles who commit criminal acts generally should be treated differently from adults.

Separate courts, detention facilities, rules, procedures, and laws were created for juveniles with the intent to protect their welfare and rehabilitate them, while protecting public safety.

In Tanzania, the Sexual Offences Special Provisions Act of Tanzania (1998) raised the minimum age of criminal responsibility from seven to 10 years. But section 15 of the penal code of Tanzania notes that: "A person under the age of seven years is not criminally responsible for any act or omission."

Separate courts, detention facilities, rules, procedures, and laws were created for juveniles with the intent to protect their welfare and rehabilitate them, while protecting public safety.

There are now similar facilities like the one in Dar es Salaam—in Tanga, Moshi, and Arusha regions. Another one is about to be opened in Mtwara.

"Children can commit crimes just like the way adults do. Children can kill, can get into drug abuse," says Officer Bwire.

A Fighting Chance

He quickly explains that the whole idea is not about punishment but to provide the children with counselling, religious and life studies, an opportunity to learn and do domestic work, primary school education, as well as sports and recreation.

Corporal Punishment in Tanzania and Zanzibar

Corporal punishment is prohibited as a disciplinary measure in penal institutions in Zanzibar under article 122(1)(d) of the Children's Act, but it is lawful in mainland Tanzania where the Law of the Child Act prohibits "torture, or other cruel, inhuman punishment or degrading treatment" (article 13) but does not explicitly prohibit corporal punishment.

"United Republic of Tanzania—Country Report,"
Global Initiative to End All Corporal Punishment of Children,
January 2011.

Charles Mkude, a lawyer working with NOLA [National Organisation for Legal Assistance] law firm, says child correctional centres are necessary in today's society but is quick to point out that they should be a last resort and that they need to have adequate facilities if they are to serve their purpose.

"They are helpful, but proper facilities are a prerequisite. Our institutions here now need assistance in forms of rehabilitation," he says. Crime experts blame tough economic situations that have left many teenagers unable to meet their basic needs for the tendency by teenagers, especially young boys, to adopt deviant behaviours.

This is corroborated by assessments done by the Legal and Human Rights Centre (LHRC) in 2003 and Envirocare in 2000, which revealed that stealing was the most frequent crime committed by juveniles.

But the officer in charge at the Upanga institution believes bad parenting is playing a significant role in juvenile delinquency.

He says: "Children brought up by irresponsible parents or in broken homes tend to commit crime in the society," he says, adding that the influence of Western culture is also a major factor.

"There is too much negative influence from the media, which is made worse by peer pressure."

Yet the major concern now is whether or not the correctional facilities in Tanzania are serving their purpose. Are they helping the children more than they are making the situation worse?

More Harm than Good

Bwire notes that the lack of funds to run the institutions is making the work difficult. And a psychologist at the University of Dar es Salaam, Dr Rebecca Sima, says locking up children in such places can do the society more harm than good.

"Correctional facilities can hurt children psychologically if the officer in charge does not handle them as a parent," says Dr Sima, who is also a professional counsellor.

She adds: "For a child under 14, such places are not good since at this age what one needs is proper parental guidance. However, it might work better for teenagers from 14 to 18 years."

Yet the major concern now is whether or not the correctional facilities in Tanzania are serving their purpose. Are they helping the children more than they are making the situation worse?

Yet for parents like Ms Georgiana Davis, whose son was sent to a correctional facility for drug abuse, even at that age, the institutions can never fix wayward teenagers.

"My son was 15 when he was sent to the institution and when he came back he was worse. He got more aggressive," says the single mother, who also admits to being a drug addict. While experts agree that correctional facilities have become very necessary, there is also a general consensus that Tanzania still has a long way to go towards reforming and upgrading its juvenile justice administration to achieve the minimum standards set by the international human rights instruments.

Ireland Should Not Be Incarcerating Children in Adult Institutions

Breda O'Brien

Breda O'Brien is a reporter for the Irish Times. *In the following viewpoint, she criticizes the recent practice of detaining juvenile offenders in adult institutions in Ireland. The boys end up in St. Patrick's Institution, a medium-security prison that has been described as brutal and inhumane. A lack of funds and the global economic downturn have been blamed for the practice, and authorities are looking at alternatives in order to protect juveniles. O'Brien contends that such alternatives are not weak on criminals but instead show compassion to young offenders.*

As you read, consider the following questions:

1. According to O'Brien, how many children aged sixteen and seventeen were committed to prison in 2010?

2. How many children are being held in protection at any one time, according to Eoin Carroll?

3. According to Emily Logan, juvenile offenders held at St. Patrick's get how many visits a week?

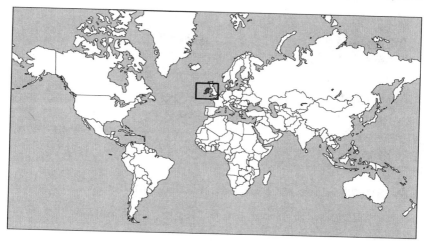

Tomorrow [November 20, 2011] is Universal Children's Day. In the Christian churches of Britain and Ireland, it is also Prisoners' Sunday. Not much overlap there, you might say. Sadly, you would be wrong.

In 2010, there were 221 children aged 16 and 17 committed to prison, including two girls. The 219 boys ended up in St Patrick's Institution, which is a medium-security prison for young males aged 16 to 21.

Children's ombudsman Emily Logan has been heavily critical of incarcerating children in institutions that also imprison adults. She is hardly alone.

A Controversial Institution

A report by the Office of the Children's Ombudsman (OCO) lists nine different groups or official bodies that have criticised St Patrick's, including everyone from the Irish Prison Chaplains to the European Committee for the Prevention of Torture and Inhuman or Degrading Treatment or Punishment and the UN [United Nations] Committee on the Rights of the Child.

Let me add one. The Whitaker commission recommended the immediate closure of St Patrick's in 1985.

It is official government policy to move children to the long-promised National Children Detention [Facility] at Oberstown in Lusk. As yet another consequence of our economic thralldom, those plans have been put on hold.

Advocacy officer of the Jesuit Centre for Faith and Justice Eoin Carroll points out that we are taking about 60 children at any one time, of whom up to 20 can be on "protection", meaning that they are locked up for 20 to 22 hours a day.

"A Humane, Child-Centred Environment"

Unsurprisingly, he called for the immediate reinstatement of the capital budget for Oberstown, "if the state is to show commitment to providing a humane, child-centred environment".

Sadly, that is unlikely to happen anytime soon. If plan A is on hold, what exactly is plan B? Emily Logan has suggested as an interim measure that the practice of holding children who are on remand in St Patrick's should stop immediately.

The detention centres currently only used for under-16s would be the obvious place to send children on remand who are over that age.

Places like Trinity House [School] are a stark contrast to the Dickensian conditions [reminiscent of Charles Dickens's novels] in St Pat's. The regime in St Pat's is a replica of an adult prison routine, with one added twist. The prisoners are not allowed to wear their own clothes.

In fact, if they end up in the special observation cell known by inmates as "the pad", they only get to wear a pair of underpants, and they can be locked in there for 23 hours.

The 2007 prison rules are absolutely clear that the special observation cell should never be used except to prevent harm to the prisoner or to others, a prison doctor must be involved and it never should be used as further punishment.

The ombudsman report, "Young People in St Patrick's Institution", says that the young prisoners are unaware of this and regard "the pad" with fear.

Sentencing Under the Children Act 2001

One of the most important provisions of the Children Act 2001 is section 96 which sets out the sentencing principles for all courts. . . . In particular, it recognises that it is desirable wherever possible to prevent interruption of a child's education, training or employment, to strengthen the relationship between children and their families and to allow children to reside in their own homes. For these reasons, it provides that any penalty imposed on the child for an offence should

- take into account as mitigating factors the child's age and level of maturity;

- interfere as little as possible with the child's education, training or employment;

- take the form most likely to maintain and promote the child's development;

- take the least restrictive form appropriate in the circumstances and in particular, be no greater than that imposed on an adult for the same offence;

- respect the principle of detention as a last resort; and

- have due regard to the interests of any victims of the child's offending.

To this has been added the requirement that the court take into account the best interests of the child during sentencing, although it also balances this with the public interest and the interests of victims.

Ursula Kilkelly, "The Irish Juvenile Justice System.
Positive Approaches to Young People in Conflict with the Law?,"
International Juvenile Justice Observatory, 2006.

A Pragmatic Approach

No doubt by now, the usual suspects will be muttering that we are not talking about children, but scumbags who need even tougher treatment, not mollycoddling.

Certainly, these 16- and 17-year-olds are among the most difficult and dysfunctional in the state.

If human compassion can't move us, though, pragmatism should.

They come from poor and often deeply dysfunctional homes. Typically, they may have learning difficulties and almost certainly dropped out of school without any qualification. Many of them have already been in care and have significant mental health and alcohol or drug problems.

In short, this child represents most of our worst nightmares, all in one undernourished body.

If human compassion can't move us, though, pragmatism should. Locking them up already costs the state a fortune. Resource teaching in primary school and intensive intervention with families could only be cheaper.

Those interventions are already too late for the prisoners, but unless we want them to become repeat offenders, leading short, desperate, miserable lives that inflict misery on many others, we have to do more than just pay lip service to rehabilitation.

Restorative Justice

The Irish Youth Justice Service through the juvenile liaison officers do sterling work diverting young people from crime. They operate a restorative justice conference scheme, where a victim can speak directly to a child about the hurt and harm that they have caused.

In some cases, there is an agreement that the child will compensate the victim or do something positive for the community.

Surely to God we could expand the role of the liaison officers to keep young people out of prison, even when they are convicted? Surely restorative justice would be of far more benefit to everyone?

Emily Logan was also at pains to point out that many of the staff in St Pat's, particularly those who teach basic skills like cooking, go far beyond the call of duty in the care they give these kids.

The problem is that they should not be there in the first place. These children get one 15-minute visit a day if they are on remand. Sentenced offenders are entitled to one 30-minute visit a week. Many families live too far away to visit. Emily Logan told me some of these so-called scumbags are crying at night because they miss their mammies.

They may be tough, hardened, scary individuals on the outside, and some of them have done very nasty things, but on the inside, they are just kids. No matter how broke we are, surely we can do better by them.

Iran, Saudi Arabia, and Sudan Should End the Juvenile Death Penalty

Human Rights Watch

Human Rights Watch (HRW) is an international human rights organization. In the following viewpoint, HRW urges the countries of Iran, Saudi Arabia, and Sudan to abolish the juvenile death penalty because it is unjust and inhumane. In recent years, a number of other countries have ceased the practice under international pressure. Iran, Saudi Arabia, and Sudan should live up to their international agreements under the Convention on the Rights of the Child and protect juvenile offenders, argues HRW.

As you read, consider the following questions:

1. What five countries were known to have executed juvenile offenders from 2005 through 2008?
2. According to Human Rights Watch, how many juvenile offenders remain under sentence of death in Iran?
3. What kinds of offenses do Saudi Arabian courts deem worthy of death sentences?

Only three countries—Iran, Saudi Arabia, and Sudan—are known to have executed an individual since the beginning of 2009 for a crime committed before age 18, Human

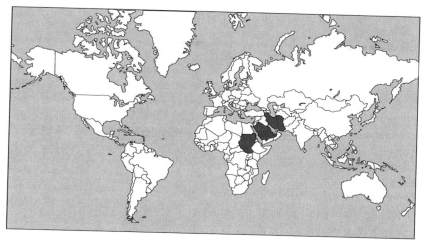

Rights Watch said today. In advance of the World Day Against the Death Penalty, October 10 [2010], Human Rights Watch called on the three countries to immediately end the practice.

The juvenile death penalty is prohibited under international law, and the prohibition is absolute. The Convention on the Rights of the Child, to which all three of the countries are parties, prohibits capital punishment for individuals who were under 18 at the time of the crime.

"Countries around the world have banned this barbaric punishment for children," said Jo Becker, children's rights advocacy director at Human Rights Watch. "Iran, Saudi Arabia, and Sudan should seize the opportunity to end this practice around the world once and for all."

In 2009, Iran executed at least five juvenile offenders, Saudi Arabia executed two, and Sudan one. This year, only one known juvenile execution has been carried out to date—in July by Iran for a crime committed at age 17.

A Disappearing Injustice

From 2005 through 2008, five countries—Iran, Saudi Arabia, Sudan, Pakistan, and Yemen—were known to have executed juvenile offenders.

"Step by step, we are coming closer to ending all executions of juvenile offenders," Becker said. "To reach this goal, countries with people on death row for crimes committed as children should immediately halt all executions of juvenile offenders and commute their sentences to bring them into line with juvenile justice standards."

According to the Children's Rights Information Network, at least twelve countries still have domestic laws that theoretically authorize the sentence. Countries that still have such laws can contribute to ending the juvenile death penalty by making sure the laws on their books ban the practice, Human Rights Watch said.

A Positive Reform

In a positive move, Sudan amended its laws in January 2010 to set 18 years as the firm age of majority nationwide. Previously, Sudan's legal system contained ambiguous provisions allowing an individual to reach the age of majority—and thus be liable to the death penalty—as young as 15. However, the December 2008 Sudanese Supreme Court decision confirming the death sentence for Abdulrahaman Zakaria Mohammed, the juvenile offender executed in 2009, was based in part on a conclusion that the prohibition of the death penalty for children did not extend to *hodud* offenses—crimes seen as being "against God." It is not clear whether the new 2010 law would affect the court's ruling regarding future *hodud* cases.

In Nigeria, over 30 juvenile offenders were on death row as of March, even though Nigeria is not known to have executed a juvenile offender since 1997. Nigeria defines the age of adulthood nationally as 17, and 12 states in northern Nigeria operate under Shari'a [Islamic religious] laws, some of which define the age of legal responsibility as younger than 17.

The United Arab Emirates (UAE) also held juvenile offenders on death row in 2010, according to local media reports. In April, the UAE Supreme Court upheld death sentences for two Emiratis and one Bangladeshi for a murder committed when each of the defendants was 17. Later in April, two other men, an Emirati and a Bangladeshi, were sentenced to death in Sharjah for a murder committed when each was 17.

Iran Executes Juvenile Offenders After They Reach 18

Iran executed at least one juvenile offender in 2010, and five in 2009.

January 21, 2009: Molla Gol Hassan, a 21-year-old Afghan citizen who at age 17 killed a fellow Afghan, Fakhr al'Din, in Iran while trying to steal money from him.

May 1, 2009: Delara Darabi, 22, for a murder she allegedly committed at age 17. Darabi had initially confessed, but later retracted her confession, saying she had hoped to protect her boyfriend from execution, because her boyfriend believed that Darabi would not be sentenced to death because she was under 18.

May 20, 2009: Ali Jafari was executed for a crime committed before age 18. The execution was reported by several Farsi news sources, but no further details on the case are available.

October 12, 2009: Behnoud Shojai, 21, hanged for a killing committed in 2005, when he was 17.

The Iranian judiciary continues to harass, prosecute, and detain human rights lawyers critical of the government's execution of juvenile offenders.

December 17, 2009: Mosleh Zamani, 23, who had been arrested at 17 in Sanandaj, Kordestan Province, on charges of abducting and raping a woman several years older with whom he was allegedly having a relationship. The appeals court judge affirmed that the sex had in fact been consensual, but still insisted that Zamani be executed to "set an example" to other young Iranians.

July 10, 2010: A person identified as Mohammad was secretly hanged in Marvdasht prison, Shiraz, in connection with the rape and murder of two young boys, Hamed Shiri and Karim Tajik, in 2007, when Mohammad was 17.

More than 100 juvenile offenders remain under sentence of death. The Iranian judiciary continues to harass, prosecute, and detain human rights lawyers critical of the government's execution of juvenile offenders. Mohammad Olyaeifard is currently serving a one-year prison sentence imposed for speaking out against the execution of his client, Behnoud Shojai, during interviews with international media. Mohammad Mostafaei, a lawyer who represented numerous juvenile offenders on death row, was forced to flee Iran in July.

Under Iranian law, majority is attained at puberty (*bulugh*), as stipulated by its interpretation of Shari'a and as specified in Iran's 1991 civil code as 15 lunar years (14 years and 5 months) for boys and 9 lunar years (8 years and 8 months) for girls. Moreover, article 82 of the Iranian penal code establishes capital punishment as the penalty for adultery crimes (*hodud*), "regardless of the age or marital status of the culprit." Further, since *hodud* crimes are seen as crimes against God, the Supreme Leader of Iran has no power to grant pardons in such cases. Punishment is fixed by the Quran and Sunnah, and, in principle cannot be altered by any authority.

In cases of murder, Iran implements "*qesas*" punishment, under which the family of the victim holds the sole power to determine whether the accused should be executed. Iranian jurisprudence considers *qesas* a personal right of the victim's family that neither the judge nor any other authority can overrule, regardless of whether the perpetrator is a juvenile. A sentence of execution is also available for the following crimes, among others: adultery, same-sex relations, apostasy, and certain drug-related offenses.

The Juvenile Death Penalty in International Law

The prohibition on the juvenile death penalty is absolute in international and customary law, and applies even in times of war. Both the Convention on the Rights of the Child, with 193 states parties, and the International Covenant on Civil and Political Rights, with 161 states parties, specifically prohibit capital punishment of persons under 18 at the time of the offense. In 1994 the UN [United Nations] Human Rights Committee stated that it considered the prohibition against executing children to be part of international customary law, and thus not open to reservations. Regional human rights treaties for Africa, the Americas, and Europe all ban the juvenile death penalty in all circumstances.

*"The Last Holdouts: Ending the Juvenile Death Penalty
in Iran, Saudi Arabia, Sudan, Pakistan, and Yemen,"
Human Rights Watch, 2008.*

During its Universal Periodic Review before the United Nations [UN] Human Rights Council in February, Iran rejected requests from member states to abolish the juvenile death penalty. Despite the absolute ban on execution of individuals charged with crimes that occurred while they were under age 18, government officials continue to insist Iran is in compliance with international law because it does not execute juvenile offenders until after they turn 18.

Saudi Arabian Justice Is Largely Based on Interpretation

Saudi Arabia executed at least two juvenile offenders in 2009.

May 12: Sultan bin Sulayman al-Muwallad, a Saudi, and Issa bin Muhammad ['Umar] Muhammad, a Chadian, for offenses committed when they were allegedly 17. The two were arrested in 2004 and held at the Medina police station, where they confessed to the abduction and rape of a child, theft, and consumption of alcohol and drugs. They were sentenced by the Medina general court in February 2008.

Saudi Arabia has neither a codified penal law establishing the acts that constitute criminal offenses nor a published official interpretation of Shari'a law, which constitutes the basis for all laws in the kingdom; instead, judges have broad discretion to interpret and apply Shari'a precepts in criminal cases.

Saudi courts have imposed the death penalty for a broad variety of offenses, including adultery, apostasy, "corruption on earth," drug trafficking, sabotage, political rebellion, and murder. The court can also impose the death penalty as a discretionary punishment *(ta'zir)* for any other acts it deems to be criminal. Under interpretations of Shari'a law prevailing in Saudi Arabia, murder and manslaughter (involuntary murder) are considered to be primarily offenses against a private right *(qisas)*. In these *qisas* cases, the deceased's family retains the right to insist on the execution of the offender, accept monetary compensation, or issue a pardon.

On November 24, 2008, the Shura Council, an appointed advisory body with some functions of a parliament, passed a measure to raise the general age of majority from 15 to 18, despite the opposition of the council's Islamic, Judicial Affairs, and Human Rights Committee. On October 4, 2010, the council again debated the age of majority in the context of a draft law on protecting children from violence and neglect. The Saudi cabinet has passed neither measure into law, and their applicability to capital punishment remains unclear. Trial judges make decisions on whether a defendant is a child based on physical signs of puberty at the time of trial and not at the time of crime. Children have been tried as adults and sentenced to death for crimes committed at age 13.

Sudan Amends the Age of Majority

On May 14, 2009, Sudan executed Abdulrahman Zakaria Mohammed in Al Fashir, North Darfur. He was 17 at the time of his trial in May 2007, when he was found guilty of murder and robbery. Gabriela Carina Knaul de Albuquerque e Silva, the UN special rapporteur on independence of judges and lawyers, said that the Supreme Court in Khartoum confirmed the death sentence in December 2008 based on two arguments. First, it found that the prohibition of the death penalty for children did not extend to *hodud* offenses. Second, the court found that the definition of a child should be drawn from the definition of "adult" provided in the Criminal Act, which was that "adult means any person whose puberty has been established by definite natural features and who has completed 15 years of age, and whoever attains 18 years of age shall be deemed an adult even if the features of puberty do not appear."

A January 2010 amendment to the Child Act set 18 years as the firm age of majority, thus addressing one of the bases on which the Supreme Court had confirmed the death sentence.

Palestinian Youths Are Being Mistreated in Israeli Detention

Harriet Sherwood

Harriet Sherwood is the Guardian's *Jerusalem correspondent. In the following viewpoint, she reports on a recent* Guardian *investigation that uncovered widespread and troubling abuse of Palestinian juveniles detained by Israeli security forces in occupied territories. Human rights organizations claim that these patterns of abuse—threats, sleep deprivation, blindfolding, and physical and verbal abuse—violate international agreements such as the fourth Geneva Convention and the United Nations Convention on the Rights of the Child. Israeli forces have denied many of these allegations, but Sherwood reports that there have been impartial witnesses who have found clear evidence of wrongdoing.*

As you read, consider the following questions:

1. According to Sherwood, how many Palestinian children are arrested by Israeli soldiers each year?

2. How many Palestinian men, women, and children does the author say have been detained under military orders since the start of Israeli occupation?

3. Under military order 1651, what is the age of criminal responsibility in the West Bank?

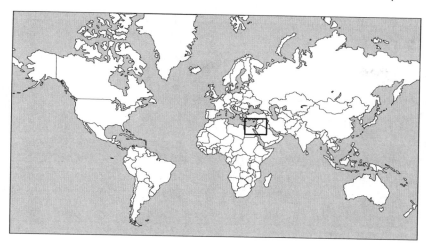

The room is barely wider than the thin, dirty mattress that covers the floor. Behind a low concrete wall is a squat toilet, the stench from which has no escape in the windowless room. The rough concrete walls deter idle leaning; the constant overhead light inhibits sleep. The delivery of food through a low slit in the door is the only way of marking time, dividing day from night.

Solitary Confinement in Cell 36

This is Cell 36, deep within Al Jalame prison in northern Israel. It is one of a handful of cells where Palestinian children are locked in solitary confinement for days or even weeks. One 16-year-old claimed that he had been kept in Cell 36 for 65 days.

The only escape is to the interrogation room where children are shackled, by hands and feet, to a chair while being questioned, sometimes for hours.

Most are accused of throwing stones at soldiers or settlers; some, of flinging Molotov cocktails; a few, of more serious offences such as links to militant organisations or using weapons. They are also pumped for information about the activities and sympathies of their classmates, relatives and neighbours.

At the beginning, nearly all deny the accusations. Most say they are threatened; some report physical violence. Verbal abuse—"You're a dog, a son of a whore"—is common. Many are exhausted from sleep deprivation. Day after day they are fettered to the chair, then returned to solitary confinement. In the end, many sign confessions that they later say were coerced.

These claims and descriptions come from affidavits given by minors to an international human rights organisation and from interviews conducted by the *Guardian*. Other cells in Al Jalame and Petah Tikva prisons are also used for solitary confinement, but Cell 36 is the one cited most often in these testimonies.

Few parents are told where their children have been taken. Minors are rarely questioned in the presence of a parent, and rarely see a lawyer before or during initial interrogation.

A Pattern of Abuse

Between 500 and 700 Palestinian children are arrested by Israeli soldiers each year, mostly accused of throwing stones. Since 2008, Defence for Children International (DCI) has collected sworn testimonies from 426 minors detained in Israel's military justice system.

Their statements show a pattern of nighttime arrests, hands bound with plastic ties, blindfolding, physical and verbal abuse, and threats. About 9% of all those giving affidavits say they were kept in solitary confinement, although there has been a marked increase to 22% in the past six months.

Few parents are told where their children have been taken. Minors are rarely questioned in the presence of a parent, and rarely see a lawyer before or during initial interrogation. Most are detained inside Israel, making family visits very difficult.

Human rights organisations say these patterns of treatment—which are corroborated by a separate study, "No Minor Matter," conducted by an Israeli group, B'Tselem—violate the international Convention on the Rights of the Child, which Israel has ratified, and the fourth Geneva Convention.

Protecting Children

Most children maintain they are innocent of the crimes of which they are accused, despite confessions and guilty pleas, said Gerard Horton of DCI. But, he added, guilt or innocence was not an issue with regard to their treatment.

"We're not saying offences aren't committed—we're saying children have legal rights. Regardless of what they're accused of, they should not be arrested in the middle of the night in terrifying raids, they should not be painfully tied up and blindfolded sometimes for hours on end, they should be informed of the right to silence and they should be entitled to have a parent present during questioning."

Mohammad Shabrawi from the West Bank town of Tulkarm was arrested last January [2011], aged 16, at about 2:30 a.m. "Four soldiers entered my bedroom and said you must come with us. They didn't say why, they didn't tell me or my parents anything," he told the *Guardian*.

Handcuffed with a plastic tie and blindfolded, he thinks he was first taken to an Israeli settlement, where he was made to kneel—still cuffed and blindfolded—for an hour on an asphalt road in the freezing dead of night. A second journey ended at about 8:00 a.m. at Al Jalame detention centre, also known as Kishon prison, amid fields close to the Nazareth to Haifa road.

The Interrogation

After a routine medical check, Shabrawi was taken to Cell 36. He spent 17 days in solitary, apart from interrogations, there and in a similar cell, No. 37, he said. "I was lonely, frightened all the time and I needed someone to talk with. I was choked from being alone. I was desperate to meet anyone, speak to anyone. . . . I was so bored that when I was out [of the cell] and saw the police, they were talking in Hebrew and I don't speak Hebrew, but I was nodding as though I understood. I was desperate to speak."

During interrogation, he was shackled. "They cursed me and threatened to arrest my family if I didn't confess," he said. He first saw a lawyer 20 days after his arrest, he said, and was charged after 25 days. "They accused me of many things," he said, adding that none of them were true.

Eventually Shabrawi confessed to membership of a banned organisation and was sentenced to 45 days. Since his release, he said, he was "now afraid of the army, afraid of being arrested." His mother said he had become withdrawn.

Another Story of Abuse

Ezz ad-Deen Ali Qadi from Ramallah, who was 17 when he was arrested last January, described similar treatment during arrest and detention. He says he was held in solitary confinement at Al Jalame for 17 days in cells 36, 37 and 38.

"I would start repeating the interrogators' questions to myself, asking myself is it true what they are accusing me of," he told the *Guardian*. "You feel the pressure of the cell. Then you think about your family, and you feel you are going to lose your future. You are under huge stress."

His treatment during questioning depended on the mood of his interrogators, he said. "If he is in a good mood, sometimes he allows you to sit on a chair without handcuffs. Or he may force you to sit on a small chair with an iron hoop behind it. Then he attaches your hands to the ring, and your legs to the chair legs. Sometimes you stay like that for four hours. It is painful.

"Sometimes they make fun of you. They ask if you want water, and if you say yes they bring it, but then the interrogator drinks it."

Ali Qadi did not see his parents during the 51 days he was detained before trial, he said, and was only allowed to see a lawyer after 10 days. He was accused of throwing stones and planning military operations, and after confessing was sentenced to six months in prison. The *Guardian* has affidavits from five other juveniles who said they were detained in solitary confinement in Al Jalame and Petah Tikva. All confessed after interrogation.

Juvenile detainees also allege harsh interrogation methods.

"Solitary confinement breaks the spirit of a child," said Horton. "Children say that after a week or so of this treatment, they confess simply to get out of the cell."

The Israeli Security Agency (ISA)—also known as Shin Bet—told the *Guardian*: "No one questioned, including minors, is kept alone in a cell as a punitive measure or in order to obtain a confession."

The Israel Prison Service did not respond to a specific question about solitary confinement, saying only "the incarceration of prisoners . . . is subject to legal examination".

Harsh Interrogation Methods

Juvenile detainees also allege harsh interrogation methods. The *Guardian* interviewed the father of a minor serving a 23-month term for throwing rocks at vehicles. Ali Odwan, from Azzoun, said his son Yahir, who was 14 when he was arrested, was given electric shocks by a Taser while under interrogation.

"I visited my son in jail. I saw marks from electric shocks on both his arms, they were visible from behind the glass. I asked him if it was from electric shocks, he just nodded. He was afraid someone was listening," Odwan said.

DCI has affidavits from three minors accused of throwing stones who claim they were given electric shocks under interrogation in 2010.

Another Azzoun youngster, Sameer Saher, was 13 when he was arrested at 2:00 a.m. "A soldier held me upside down and took me to a window and said: 'I want to throw you from the window.' They beat me on the legs, stomach, face," he said.

His interrogators accused him of stone-throwing and demanded the names of friends who had also thrown stones. He was released without charge about 17 hours after his arrest. Now, he said, he has difficulty sleeping for fear "they will come at night and arrest me".

In response to questions about alleged ill treatment, including electric shocks, the ISA said: "The claims that Palestinian minors were subject to interrogation techniques that include beatings, prolonged periods in handcuffs, threats, kicks, verbal abuse, humiliation, isolation and prevention of sleep are utterly baseless. . . . Investigators act in accordance with the law and unequivocal guidelines which forbid such actions."

Israeli military law has been applied in the West Bank since Israel occupied the territory more than 44 years ago.

The *Guardian* has also seen rare audiovisual recordings of the interrogations of two boys, aged 14 and 15, from the village of Nabi Salih, the scene of weekly protests against nearby settlers. Both are visibly exhausted after being arrested in the middle of the night. Their interrogations, which begin at about 9:30 a.m., last four and five hours.

Neither is told of their legal right to remain silent, and both are repeatedly asked leading questions, including whether named people have incited them to throw stones. At one point, as one boy rests his head on the table, the interrogator flicks at him, shouting: "Lift your head, you." During the other boy's interrogation, one questioner repeatedly slams a clenched fist into his own palm in a threatening gesture. The boy breaks down in tears, saying he was due to take an exam at school that morning. "They're going to fail me, I'm going to lose the year," he sobs.

In neither case was a lawyer present during their interrogation.

Trouble in the West Bank

Israeli military law has been applied in the West Bank since Israel occupied the territory more than 44 years ago. Since then, more than 700,000 Palestinian men, women and children have been detained under military orders.

Under military order 1651, the age of criminal responsibility is 12 years, and children under the age of 14 face a maximum of six months in prison.

However, children aged 14 and 15 could, in theory, be sentenced up to 20 years for throwing an object at a moving vehicle with the intent to harm. In practice, most sentences range between two weeks and 10 months, according to DCI.

In September 2009, a special juvenile military court was established. It sits at Ofer, a military prison outside Jerusalem, twice a week. Minors are brought into court in leg shackles and handcuffs, wearing brown prison uniforms. The proceedings are in Hebrew with intermittent translation provided by Arabic-speaking soldiers.

The Israel Prison Service told the *Guardian* that the use of restraints in public places was permitted in cases where "there is reasonable concern that the prisoner will escape, cause damage to property or body, or will damage evidence or try to dispose of evidence".

Arbitrary Detention and Detention of Children in the West Bank

Israeli military justice authorities arbitrarily detained Palestinians who advocated nonviolent protest against Israeli settlements and the route of the separation barrier. In January [2011] a military appeals court increased the prison sentence of Abdallah Abu Rahme, from the village of Bil'in, to 16 months in prison on charges of inciting violence and organizing illegal demonstrations, largely on the basis of coerced statements of children.

In a positive development, in September the Israeli military issued an order raising the age of majority for Palestinians to 18 years; previously 16- and 17-year-olds had been treated as adults under the security regime. Human rights groups reported, however, that Israeli authorities continued to sentence Palestinians according to their age at the time of sentencing even if they were children at the time of the offense, and documented cases in which Israeli authorities arrested children in their homes at night, at gunpoint, questioned them without a family member or a lawyer, and coerced them to sign confessions in Hebrew, which they did not understand.

As of September . . . Israel detained 164 Palestinian children under 18 years old, and also held 272 Palestinians in administrative detention without charge; Israel released at least 9 administrative detainees, but no children, in the prisoner exchange.

"World Report 2012," Human Rights Watch, January 2012.

The *Guardian* witnessed a case this month [in January 2012] in which two boys, aged 15 and 17, admitted entering Israel illegally, throwing Molotov cocktails and stones, starting a fire which caused extensive damage, and vandalising property. The prosecution asked for a sentence to reflect the defendants' "nationalistic motives" and to act as a deterrent.

The older boy was sentenced to 33 months in jail; the younger one, 26 months. Both were sentenced to an additional 24 months suspended and were fined 10,000 shekels (£1,700). Failure to pay the fine would mean an additional 10 months in prison.

British Witnesses Report Distressing Scenes

Several British parliamentary delegations have witnessed child hearings at Ofer over the past year. Alf Dubs reported back to the House of Lords last May, saying: "We saw a 14-year-old and a 15-year-old, one of them in tears, both looking absolutely bewildered. . . . I do not believe this process of humiliation represents justice. I believe that the way in which these young people are treated is in itself an obstacle to the achievement by Israel of a peaceful relationship with the Palestinian people."

Lisa Nandy, MP [member of Parliament] for Wigan, who witnessed the trial of a shackled 14-year-old at Ofer last month, found the experience distressing. "In five minutes he had been found guilty of stone-throwing and was sentenced to nine months. It was shocking to see a child being put through this process. It's difficult to see how a [political] solution can be reached when young people are being treated in this manner. They end up with very little hope for their future and very angry about their treatment."

Horton said a guilty plea was "the quickest way to get out of the system". If the children say their confession was coerced, "that provides them with a legal defence—but because they're denied bail they will remain in detention longer than if they had simply pleaded guilty".

An expert opinion written by Graciela Carmon, a child psychiatrist and member of Physicians for Human Rights, in May 2011, said that children were particularly vulnerable to providing a false confession under coercion.

"Although some detainees understand that providing a confession, despite their innocence, will have negative repercussions in the future, they nevertheless confess as the immediate mental and/or physical anguish they feel overrides the future implications, whatever they may be."

Nearly all the cases documented by DCI ended in a guilty plea and about three-quarters of the convicted minors were transferred to prisons inside Israel. This contravenes article 76 of the fourth Geneva Convention, which requires children and adults in occupied territories to be detained within the territory.

A Categorical Denial

The Israeli Defense Forces (IDF), responsible for arrests in the West Bank and the military judicial system, said last month that the military judicial system was "underpinned by a commitment to ensure the rights of the accused, judicial impartiality and an emphasis on practising international legal norms in incredibly dangerous and complex situations".

The ISA said its employees acted in accordance with the law, and detainees were given the full rights for which they were eligible, including the right to legal counsel and visits by the Red Cross. "The ISA categorically denies all claims with regard to the interrogation of minors. In fact, the complete opposite is true—the ISA guidelines grant minors special protections needed because of their age."

Mark Regev, spokesman for the Israeli prime minister, Benjamin Netanyahu, told the *Guardian*: "If detainees believe they have been mistreated, especially in the case of minors . . . it's very important that these people, or people representing them, come forward and raise these issues. The test of a democracy is how you treat people incarcerated, people in jail, and especially so with minors."

Stone-throwing, he added, was a dangerous activity that had resulted in the deaths of an Israeli father and his infant son last year.

Human rights groups are concerned about the long-term impact of detention on Palestinian minors.

"Rock-throwing, throwing Molotov cocktails and other forms of violence is unacceptable, and the security authorities have to bring it to an end when it happens."

The Long-Term Effects of Detention

Human rights groups are concerned about the long-term impact of detention on Palestinian minors. Some children initially exhibit a degree of bravado, believing it to be a rite of passage, said Horton. "But when you sit with them for an hour or so, under this veneer of bravado are children who are fairly traumatised." Many of them, he said, never want to see another soldier or go near a checkpoint. Does he think the system works as a deterrent? "Yes, I think it does."

According to Nader Abu Amsha, the director of the YMCA in Beit Sahour, near Bethlehem, which runs a rehabilitation programme for juveniles, "families think that when the child is released, it's the end of the problem. We tell them this is the beginning".

Following detention many children exhibit symptoms of trauma: nightmares, mistrust of others, fear of the future, feelings of helplessness and worthlessness, obsessive-compulsive behaviour, bed-wetting, aggression, withdrawal and lack of motivation.

The Israeli authorities should consider the long-term effects, said Abu Amsha. "They don't give attention to how this might continue the vicious cycle of violence, of how this might increase hatred. These children come out of this process with a lot of anger. Some of them feel the need for revenge.

"You see children who are totally broken. It's painful to see the pain of these children, to see how much they are squeezed by the Israeli system."

Argentina Considers Lowering the Age of Criminal Responsibility

Marcela Valente

Marcela Valente is a correspondent for Inter Press Service, an international news agency. In the following viewpoint, Valente chronicles a recent push in Argentina to lower the criminal age of responsibility. According to Valente, the murder of an Argentinean man at the hands of minors has sparked a national debate around juvenile crime. At what age should a minor be held criminally responsible? Valente explains that Argentina does not have a separate criminal justice system for juveniles, and critics of lowering the age of responsibility argue that there are better alternatives to incarceration for juvenile offenders altogether. Valente maintains that proposals for lowering the age of responsibility have brought awareness to a system in need of reform and have fueled public discourse.

As you read, consider the following questions:

1. According to Valente, why is it important to have a separate justice system for juveniles?
2. What is the age of criminal responsibility in Argentina?

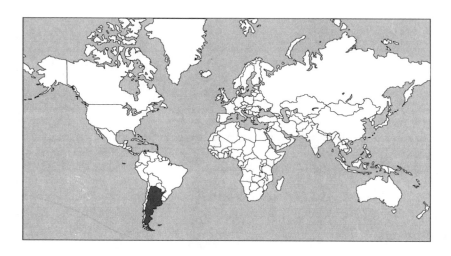

3. How does the UN Convention on the Rights of the Child define a child, according to the viewpoint?

The recent murder of a man allegedly at the hands of teen-agers has sparked a heated debate in Argentina between advocates of lowering the age of criminal responsibility and those in favour of a juvenile justice system in line with the United Nations Convention on the Rights of the Child.

A National Debate

The incident that revived the debate occurred on Oct. 20 [2008], when burglars who broke into a house in the upscale Buenos Aires district of San Isidro shot and killed the owner and left his 17-year-old son seriously wounded.

The controversy broke out as soon as it was reported that two minors had been arrested in connection with the case.

Daniel Scioli, governor of the eastern province of Buenos Aires, called for an "in-depth debate towards reducing the age of criminal responsibility of minors involved in serious offences." He pointed out that other Latin American countries, such as Brazil, Ecuador, Mexico and Paraguay, have already done so.

But in those countries and in almost all of Latin America there is a special justice system for juvenile offenders that affords children and adolescents due process protections and the right to defence when they are accused of a crime, under a specific regime that is entirely different from the criminal justice system that applies to adults.

Argentina lacks a special [justice] system for minors.

Most countries in the region have established a statutory minimum age under which minors are not considered legally responsible for their actions, which ranges from 12 to 14. But 18 is still the age of criminal responsibility.

In Argentina, by contrast, young people are not considered legally liable until the age of 16, but 16- and 17-year-old offenders are frequently transferred to adult criminal courts—running counter to international standards—or are held in juvenile detention centres for longer periods than their offences actually warrant.

The reason for this is that Argentina lacks a special system for minors, as stipulated by the Convention on the Rights of the Child (CRC) adopted by the United Nations in 1989 and ratified by Argentina in 1990. Moreover, still in force in the country is a decree issued by the 1976–1983 dictatorship, which grants judges a great deal of discretion and thus increases the possibility of arbitrary rulings.

Is Change Necessary?

This has led experts on juvenile justice issues and lawmakers to recommend that the obsolete decree be repealed without delay and a new juvenile court system be implemented in its place, to provide alternatives to imprisonment, lighter sentences, and access to schooling and health care, among other measures.

Consulted by IPS [Inter Press Service], Gimol Pinto, a specialist in legal reform and child welfare with the United Nations Children's Fund (UNICEF), said that in most countries of the region the minimum age for a person to be tried under juvenile criminal law ranges from 12 to 14 years.

In Argentina there are currently 14 bills proposing the creation of a juvenile justice system, all of which set the minimum age at which minors can be held legally responsible for their actions at around 14.

Pinto added that in 2007 the Committee on the Rights of the Child, which monitors implementation of the CRC by signatory states, considered that 12 was too young an age for children to be criminally prosecuted, and that the ideal minimum age would be between 14 and 16.

Creating a Juvenile Justice System

In Argentina there are currently 14 bills proposing the creation of a juvenile justice system, all of which set the minimum age at which minors can be held legally responsible for their actions at around 14. The UN convention defines children as "every human being below the age of eighteen years."

The country cannot fully "comply with the Convention unless it reforms its criminal law system, and this reform must involve a discussion not only of the minimum age (of criminal responsibility), but also of the need to put in place a juvenile justice system that considers depriving juvenile offenders of their liberty as a measure of last resort and applies it only for the shortest time possible," Pinto said.

In 2005, prompted by reports presented to the Inter-American Court of Human Rights of cases of juvenile offenders who were sentenced to life imprisonment, Argentina's Supreme Court ruled that anyone under 18 who commits a serious offence must receive a penalty in accordance with the scale of attempted crimes as provided for under the criminal code, which establishes lighter sentences.

But legislators and jurists insist that what is needed is a specific justice system for minors. Officials close to Governor Scioli explained that what he was referring to was precisely such systems, in order to deal with offences involving minors with more appropriate mechanisms.

Buenos Aires police chief Daniel Salcedo maintained that in his jurisdiction young people are involved in approximately one million crimes a year, of which only 1,000 to 1,200 a month are reported.

Finding Effective Solutions

However, experts on children's issues, jurists and Catholic activists say that most juvenile delinquents have not committed serious offences, like murder or kidnapping, and that what is needed, rather than a tougher law enforcement approach, are social policies aimed at strengthening family ties and keeping kids in school.

The cry for a tougher law enforcement approach to minors voiced by thousands of San Isidro residents at a demonstration held shortly after the Oct. 20 murder in that neighbourhood was seen by Nora Schulman, head of the Argentine committee for monitoring and implementation of the Convention on the Rights of the Child, as "a step backwards."

Referring to the demand for a reduction in the age of criminal responsibility, Schulman told IPS that "we see this as a knee-jerk reaction to social pressure. In the absence of effective public safety policies, the chain breaks at the weakest link, and apparently the easiest way to solve things is to lock kids up at increasingly younger ages." But this demand goes against some advances seen at the national level, she said.

"The national government has shown that it is willing to acknowledge the problem, and to that end has just completed

"There's so much I want to do with my life...before I reach the age of criminal responsibility, that is," cartoon by Len Hawkins. www.CartoonStock.com.

an assessment of the situation," she said, referring to a report ... released in October by the Ministry of Social Development and UNICEF.

Recommendations for Reform

According to the report, in 2007 there were a total of 6,294 juvenile offenders and suspects, 90 percent of whom were male, 72 percent of whom were above the age of 16, and 70 percent of whom were involved in crimes against property, although in two-thirds of these cases no weapons were used.

The study—which does not mention the age of criminal responsibility—also maintains that "a legal reform is not essential to put an end to detentions in police stations, overcrowded conditions and abuses in institutions, or the use of deprivation of liberty as a measure of first, instead of last, resort."

The report's authors also recommend creating "a specific criminal justice system" for children and adolescents, with alternative programmes, institutions appropriate to their age, and the "commitment of handing down prison sentences only as a measure of last resort and for the shortest period of time possible."

These recommendations are within the spirit of the Convention on the Rights of the Child that Argentina incorporated into its constitution in 1994. They are also innovative measures, considering the high degree of discretion that judges currently have, which means that minors brought to trial are left at the mercy of the judge who hears their case.

England's Juvenile Justice System Is Cruel and Counterproductive

Rod Morgan

Rod Morgan was chairman of the Youth Justice Board for England and Wales from 2004 to 2007. In the following viewpoint, he maintains that the juvenile justice system in England is counterproductive and creates lifelong offenders. Morgan argues that instead of "getting tough on crime," policy makers should be focusing on humane and effective policies that don't criminalize antisocial behavior and creating a new agency to develop community-oriented institutions instead of juvenile detention centers. He also urges policy makers to consider raising the age of criminal responsibility in England.

As you read, consider the following questions:

1. How many more children were there in custody in 2007 than there were in the beginning of the 1990s, according to Morgan?

2. How much does Morgan say it costs to keep a minor in juvenile detention for a year?

3. According to Morgan, how long on average does a juvenile offender spend in custody?

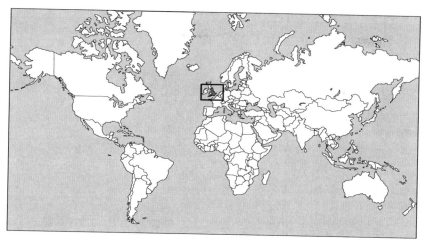

W here was law and order in the 2010 election? During the campaign, there were arguments about civil liberties, identity cards and immigration control. But the election was the first in over 30 years in which law and order barely figured. This is even more striking given that 2010 will go down as a political turning point.

The major cuts in public spending in the policy pipeline provide an opportunity for us to stop . . . criminalising and locking up so many children and young people.

The Evolution of Attitudes on Crime

In 1979, the Conservative Party made law and order central to its drive for power, capturing significant numbers of core Labour voters. In 1997, New Labour reversed the trick, overtaking the Tories on the right and distancing itself from Old Labour's law-challenging radicalism. Most of New Labour's effort went on the first half of its populist slogan "Tough on crime; tough on the causes of crime". Perhaps 2010 will signal a welcome cooling of the law-and-order party-political arms race.

No serious analyst of law-and-order policies believes that either the welter of new legislation that has afflicted our criminal justice system or the locking up of increasing numbers of offenders has made us safer in our beds at night. There is general agreement that the time has come to roll back our heavy use of criminal justice interventions and stop talking up the potency of criminal law to solve our social ills.

On 30 March [2010], just over a month before polling day, Iain Duncan Smith argued in a speech at the Attlee Foundation in London that we could not "arrest our way out of our problems". At the same event, by contrast, Chris Grayling promised "robust policing", but he was not heard of for the rest of the campaign. Grayling may not get it, but most politicians now do. They privately agree with the Treasury that a grave financial crisis should not go to waste.

The major cuts in public spending in the policy pipeline provide an opportunity for us to stop doing a few things we should never have done—chief among them criminalising and locking up so many children and young people, thereby grooming a new generation of long-term adult criminals from whose depredations we will all suffer.

The trend is clear. Even though the volume of crimes, including those for which young people are responsible, has fallen since the mid-1990s, by 2007 there were more than twice as many children in custody as at the beginning of the 1990s. The increase is not explained by a corresponding rise in serious crime by children. Events such as the murder of James Bulger [a two-year-old who was abducted and killed by two ten-year-old boys] in February 1993 or the torture of two boys in Edlington, South Yorkshire, in April 2009, are thankfully rare. In that sense, Britain is no more broken today than it was 20 years ago.

Paying the Price

Nor should we get hung up about offensive, antisocial behaviour committed by young people. That may have got worse, but no one seriously believes that the problem is best solved by putting already disaffected and typically disadvantaged youths behind bars. At roughly £100,000 a year, this costs more than three times as much as sending a child to Eton [a boarding school for teenage boys], and the outcome is not an enhanced prospect of becoming prime minister, but typically a lifelong relationship with the revolving door of Pentonville [a men's prison]. As the former Conservative home secretary David Waddington confessed, it is an expensive way of making bad people worse.

So, how to save taxpayers money and better protect us from being victimised? It is a good first step that the plan to build a 360-bed young offender institution (YOI) outside Leicester has been scrapped. The proposal was undesirable and unnecessary. The youth custody population of England and Wales has fallen in the past two years from 3,000 to roughly 2,200. The surplus capacity this creates should allow the Youth Justice Board [for England and Wales], which commissions custodial places for under-18s, to avoid unsuitable establishments. Indeed, it should be thinking about a completely different residential model.

Preventing youth crime involves . . . promoting positive, law-abiding opportunities and working with families as well as individual offenders—not further dislocating already fragile relationships.

Proposed Reforms

The new government should now also do the following. First, a new agency should be created, separate from the prison service, to manage all accommodation for young offenders—the local authority secure homes, the commercially run secure training centres and the YOIs. This would make for coherent national planning, which is at present lacking.

Juvenile Crime in England and Wales

Key Facts:

- Number of under-18s in custody in 2010: 2,209.

- Total number of recorded offences committed by youth in 2007/8: 277,986.

- Total cost of dealing with young offenders to the criminal justice services 2008/9: £4 billion a year.

- Every year an estimated 70,000 school-age children enter the youth justice system.

- Nearly half (42%) of first time offenders are young adults.

- More than a fifth of under-18-year-olds in custody were there on remand.

- The number of 15–17-year-olds in prison has more than doubled over the last ten years.

- In March 2007 there were 2,413 15–17-year-olds in prison.

- In March 2007 there were 229 12–15-year-olds in privately run secure training centres.

TAKEN FROM: Lara Natale, "Factsheet—Youth Crime in England and Wales," Civitas, 2010.

This new agency should consider piloting a community-oriented institution along the lines of the proposed young offenders academy investigated over the past three years by a working party with the Foyer Federation, the support agency for youngsters making the transition to adulthood. We must keep the secure homes for younger children provided by local authorities. They are expensive, but they provide the sort of one-to-one care needed by children who have done dreadful things but are often both neglected and disturbed. In addition, we must explore an alternative model to the big YOI, an outmoded tool that should have been consigned to the penal dustbin.

Most of the cost of youth custody should be transferred from central government to the local authorities from which the young people come. This proposition has been pondered indecisively in Whitehall [referring to the British government] for several years. It must now be done. It would be the best way to give an incentive to the local authorities to invest in crime-preventive community programmes (research shows that confidence in these programmes is critical in persuading sentencers to avoid the use of custody). If this happened, a question mark would hang over the continued need for the Youth Justice Board.

The thousands of young people locked up each year spend, on average, 14 weeks in custody. It is wrong that a high proportion of them are held far from home, and unsurprising that the overwhelming majority are reconvicted within 12 months of getting out. Preventing youth crime involves determining responsibility and fixing consequences. But it also involves promoting positive, law-abiding opportunities and working with families as well as individual offenders—not further dislocating already fragile relationships. None of these processes is best achieved by transporting teenage offenders to large, distant, prison-like institutions.

Too Much Too Soon

Finally, the conviction on 24 May [2010] of two boys aged ten and 11 on a charge of attempted rape of an eight-year-old girl should lead the government to reconsider the age of criminal responsibility. It is not in the interests of any child, either victim or offender, or society at large, that children as young as this undergo adversarial criminal justice proceedings. Such matters are, if necessary, better dealt with by the family courts and child-care proceedings.

Law-and-order services, which cost just under 6 per cent of overall public expenditure, are not going to be among the heaviest hit in the period 2011–2014. Policing, which claims the largest share of the pot, is too politically sensitive for that. But things are nonetheless going to be tough for frontline practitioners. There will be significant cuts. This makes it imperative that we shift the centre of expenditure gravity from that which is totemic to something that has a prospect of working.

Periodical and Internet Sources Bibliography

The following articles have been selected to supplement the diverse views presented in this chapter.

Rishawn Biddle	"Juvenile Abuse," *American Spectator*, March 11, 2011.
Jeri Clausing	"When Should a School Call in the Police? Handcuffed 6-Year-Old Fuels Debate," *Toronto Star*, April 18, 2012.
Sarah Dingle	"Call for Radical Intervention on Juvenile Justice," ABC News, May 25, 2011. www.abc.net.au.
Gulf News (Dubai)	"Young Aboriginal Inmates Deemed 'National Crisis,'" June 21, 2011.
Haaretz (Israel)	"Continuing Neglect of Juveniles," March 7, 2011.
Adele Horin	"Conferences Could Replace Jail for Young Sex Offenders," *Sydney Morning Herald*, January 24, 2012.
Constance Jamet and Marc de Boni	"France Calls for Reform After Murder of Girl, 13," *Le Figaro* (France), November 23, 2011.
Fadela Slamdien	"Juvenile Criminals Fall Through Chasm of State Ineptitude," *West Cape News* (Cape Town, South Africa), June 21, 2010.
USA Today	"Dealing with Child-on-Child Sex Abuse Not One Size Fits All," January 7, 2012.
Tom Wright	"Kashmir Youth Detained Illegally, Report Says," *Wall Street Journal*, November 16, 2011.

GLOBALVIEWPOINTS

CHAPTER 4

Juvenile Justice System Reforms

Federal Legislation Tough on Young Criminals

Anna Mehler Paperny

Anna Mehler Paperny is a reporter for the Globe and Mail. *In the following viewpoint, she scrutinizes a recent legislative proposal by the Conservative government in Canada to get tougher on juvenile crime. The new law would expand the crimes for which juveniles can be incarcerated and the amount of time they spend in custody. Critics of the proposed legislation argue that such a strategy is too expensive and has been proven ineffective in other countries, such as the United States. Imposing tougher sentences and imprisoning more young offenders, asserts Paperny, will only lead to more recidivism and will take a serious economic toll on Canada's economy.*

As you read, consider the following questions:

1. According to Paperny, how many more convicted teens are sent into custody in Canada than in England or Wales?

2. How many custody sentences does the author say were meted out to Canadian youth in 2004?

3. According to international studies, how much less likely are young people who are put behind bars to get a job once they get out compared to those who don't go to prison?

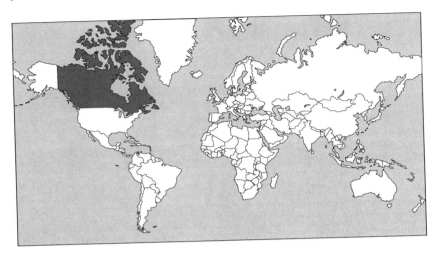

Canada incarcerates more convicted youth than almost any similarly industrialized country.

And new federal crime legislation is poised to drive those numbers higher, even though imprisoned teens are statistically less likely to get jobs after they're released and, if anything, are more likely to re-offend.

Years after enacting laws that have been successful in reducing youth incarceration rates, Canada still sends five times more of its convicted teens into custody than England and Wales, according to data obtained from the British Ministry of Justice and Statistics Canada's justice arm.

A Debate on the Juvenile Justice System in Canada

At the crux of the debate is how to treat Canada's youngest criminals. They represent a complex cohort in a diverse country, spread out across divergent provincial justice systems. The current tool is the nine-year-old Youth Criminal Justice Act [YCJA], a law meant to strike a delicate balance between getting tough on repeat, violent offenders while ensuring other youth charged with crimes stayed out of jail.

It has succeeded in lowering incarceration rates, although Canada is still high compared with other OECD [Organisation for Economic Co-operation and Development] countries—a comparison many argue is misleading given differences in the way countries measure those stats.

But even its proponents argue the resources needed to create alternative sentencing and rehabilitation, let alone prevent teens from getting in trouble in the first place, aren't there. Critics point to harrowing cases of youth crime and argue the law's too lax. As it is, the system's still torn between a focus on punishment and deterrence on one hand, and prevention and rehabilitation on the other.

During the recent federal election campaign [for the 2010 election], Prime Minister Stephen Harper promised to pass an omnibus crime bill in the first 100 days of Parliament. Among those 11 pieces of legislation is Bill C-4 [also known as Sébastien's Law], which would expand the crimes for which youth can be incarcerated and the amount of time they can spend in custody. It also introduces principles of "deterrence and denunciation" as elements influencing the kind of sentence someone receives.

The omnibus bill's jail-intensive emphasis confounds criminologists on both sides of the border: As Canada goes the tough-on-crime route when it comes to young offenders, many U.S. states are going in the opposite direction. They've found this strategy doesn't work and, moreover, it's bankrupting them by driving stratospheric costs to feed, house and monitor prisoners who often spend their lives in the penal system.

The Many Costs of Incarceration

The problem with locking young people up is that, eventually, they get out. And when they do, they have a larger portion of their lives ahead of them than older offenders.

The costs go beyond the price to build jails and feed and house people inside them: Young, working-age Canadians should be driving the economy as the country braces for the demographic crunch of aging baby boomers. If these young people spend their lives behind bars instead of in the work force, they act as an economic drain instead.

"It is actually a question of economic competitiveness," said Queen's University criminologist Nick Bala. "Are we going to have a significant portion of our youth essentially written off? I don't think we can afford to do that."

Going to jail taught Oluwasegun Akinsanya a lesson. Kind of.

"It's like Criminal University," he said. "All you do in jail is sit down and talk—what he did, what he did, what he did. You realize, 'Hey, that's an opportunity.' You learn from their mistakes. You'll come back and do a better version."

While studies have shown young, still-developing brains are more receptive to rehabilitative attempts, they're also more susceptible to the malfeasant influence of fellow offenders, experts say. Even if teens are in jail for a short period of time, says B.C. [British Columbia] children's advocate Mary Ellen Turpel-Lafond, "that recycles the kids into more offending."

It was the fall of 2004, Mr. Akinsanya was 16 years old and in Brookside Youth Centre—sentenced to a month in jail for precisely the kind of crime for which the Youth Criminal Justice Act was supposed to keep teens out of custody: He breached a bail condition.

"Those were the worst 30 days of my life."

His custody sentence was one of 8,610 meted out to Canadian youth that year, for crimes ranging from homicide and major assault to break-and-enter, impaired driving and breach of parole.

The Risks of Re-Offending

When Mr. Akinsanya got out, "I just went on a rampage . . . doing anything and everything I could to get my hands on money."

It escalated until the evening of April 20, 2006.

Mr. Akinsanya cranes his head around to show the thin white scar worming its way around the back of his neck where someone stabbed him near Keele Street and Wilson Avenue in northwest Toronto. Mr. Akinsanya grabbed the knife—a "dagger," he calls it, spreading thumb and pinky finger across the diameter of the paper dinner plate balanced on his knee—and "I disarmed him, and then I stabbed him, and then he died."

Youth justice is a prickly issue: The way a community polices, prosecutes, sentences and rehabilitates young people prods at sensitive societal sensibilities.

Mr. Akinsanya showed up for a Grade 12 math test the next day—"I didn't want to fail"—and then took off. Four days later, he turned himself in.

He bounced from Maplehurst to the Don Jail [the Toronto Jail], Millhaven Institution and Fenbrook penitentiary. But repeatedly, he says how lucky he was: When he got out, he stayed out.

"I said, 'Enough is enough,' and streamlined my way into something positive," he said. "I didn't really have it bad. But a lot of people do."

Crime and Punishment for Minors

Youth justice is a prickly issue: The way a community polices, prosecutes, sentences and rehabilitates young people prods at sensitive societal sensibilities. And concerns about the effects of crime and incarceration on malleable minds have tied criminologists and policy makers in knots for decades.

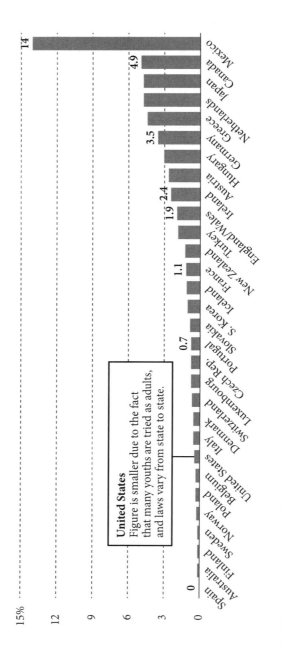

Youths as a Percentage of the Total Prison Population

This graph represents Organisation for Economic Co-operation and Development (OECD) member countries. It is based on data from Statistics Canada, Youth Justice Board for England and Wales, OECD, and the International Centre for Prison Studies.

United States
Figure is smaller due to the fact that many youths are tried as adults, and laws vary from state to state.

TAKEN FROM: Anna Mehler Paperny and Matthew Bambach, "Federal Legislation Tough on Young Criminals," *Globe and Mail*, July 18, 2011.

International studies have indicated young people who are put behind bars are 11 per cent less likely to get a job once they get out, compared with those who don't go to prison, even once researchers account for pre-conviction differences in background and upbringing.

At the same time, young people who are incarcerated are no less likely to re-offend than those who serve alternative sentences in the community—if anything, recidivism is more likely.

"Adolescents are more amenable to rehabilitation than adult offenders," Prof. Bala argues. "[But] if a young person commits one offence and then re-offends, that's going to be a life of crime."

The Youth Criminal Justice Act created a new category for violent, high-risk young offenders, providing longer, adult sentences for some; at the same time, it gave police and others more discretion and flexibility in handling cases of young offenders. Jail time was intended as a last, and largely undesirable, resort.

Some point to the subsequent decline in Canada's youth incarceration rates and argue the law has succeeded. Critics say the act as it stands now lets minors get away with too much, while failing to provide justice for victims.

Current and Proposed Legislation

That's where the federal government's Bill C-4 comes in.

"We need to strengthen the way our young offenders system deals with violent and repeat young offenders," said Justice Ministry spokeswoman Pamela Stephens. "We remain unwavering in our commitment to fighting crime and protecting Canadians so that our communities are safe places for people to live, raise their families and do business."

Justice Minister Rob Nicholson would not comment.

While this has been cheered by victims' rights organizations, others say it will do little for public safety. Instead, child advocates would like to see funding for programs to reinte-grate youth back into the community.

There's no question some youth need to be behind bars, child advocate Ms. Turpel-Lafond said. "But the question re-ally is, 'Is that the majority of the cases we have in custody?'"

Youth Criminal Justice Act [YCJA]:

- Introduced in 1998, passed by the House of Commons in 2002.

- Encourages extrajudicial measures as "often the most appropriate and effective way to address youth crime," especially in cases of nonviolent or first-time offend-ers.

- Included a clause stressing the circumstances of ab-original youth be considered at sentencing.

- Allowed provinces, if they chose, to lower the age at which a youth can receive an adult sentence to 14 from 16.

- Changed sentencing procedures to facilitate commu-nity supervision at the end of a custody sentence.

- Custody sentences are a last resort, and only given out if: the youth has committed a violent offence; has failed to comply with at least two noncustodial sen-tences; has committed an indictable offence and has "several findings of guilt;" or under "aggravating cir-cumstances."

Bill C-4—Sébastien's Law:

- Named after 19-year-old murder victim Sébastien Lacasse; introduced by the federal Conservatives last fall [2010]; part of this government's omnibus crime bill pledged to be put through within its first 100 days.

- Would make the following changes to the YCJA:

- Expand definition of "violent offence" to include reckless behaviour endangering public safety.

- Expand the crimes eligible for pretrial detention to include people accused of serious property crimes.

- Require police to keep a record of any extrajudicial measures (alternative measures outside the court process) imposed on young people, so their "criminal tendencies can be documented."

- Authorize courts to punish youth who've already had multiple extrajudicial measures to impose jail sentences.

- Require Crown [Canadian Ministry] to consider seeking an adult sentence for young offenders 14 to 17 years old convicted of murder, attempted murder, manslaughter or aggravated sexual assault.

- Establish deterrence and denunciation as sentencing principles.

China Plans Major Reforms of Its Juvenile Justice System

Frank Ching

Frank Ching is a journalist. In the following viewpoint, he outlines several proposed reforms to China's Criminal Procedure Law, concluding that some of them may be double-edged swords. Ching praises proposed reforms to the juvenile justice system, which will exempt certain juvenile offenders from prosecution and incarceration, as well as seal the arrest and incarceration records of most juvenile offenders. He urges policy makers to take seriously the feedback on the proposed reforms and drop objectionable provisions to the new law.

As you read, consider the following questions:

1. According to Ching, is torture legal in China?
2. When was the first version of China's Criminal Procedure Law passed, according to Ching?
3. How many ESS (endangering state security) crimes were prosecuted in China in 2010, according to the author?

Reform of the Chinese legal system is desperately needed but the draft of large-scale amendments to the Criminal Procedure Law shows that the current exercise in law reform is potentially a double-edged sword.

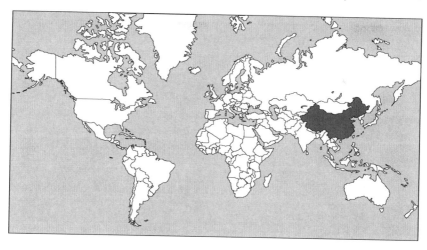

Commendably, the draft law moves much closer toward the accused having a right to silence by recognizing the right against self-incrimination, saying "no person may be forced to prove his or her own guilt."

Key Reforms

Traditionally, China has emphasized confessions and torture is still commonplace. In fact, there have been highly publicized cases where men serving prison terms for murder after confessing under torture were released when the "victims" turned up alive.

The new emphasis on the prosecution to build a case by gathering evidence and calling witnesses suggests that Chinese courtrooms are going to become livelier places.

As a result, the current draft states: "The use of torture or extortion to obtain a confession and the use of other illegal means to collect evidence shall be strictly prohibited."

Instead, it declares, "The onus of proof that a defendant is guilty shall be on the public prosecutor."

A new article has also been introduced that recognizes the right of spouses not to testify against each other. This right is extended also to the parents or children of the defendant. Other witnesses, however, may be compelled to appear.

The new emphasis on the prosecution to build a case by gathering evidence and calling witnesses suggests that Chinese courtrooms are going to become livelier places. Currently, it is rare for witnesses to be called to testify and then be subjected to cross-examination by lawyers for the opposing side.

As a result, trials tend to be brief affairs, often decided in a few hours. If the draft law is passed, we are likely to see longer trials and more fireworks in the courtroom.

The draft refers to "open trial cases" but does not define them. At present, many trials are theoretically "open" but closed in reality. And if trials are not open to the public and the media, there is no way of monitoring the extent to which the criminal procedure law is being observed.

Moreover, the new law says nothing about immunity for legal practitioners. Currently, lawyers are subject to arrest on charges of coaching their clients to lie in court, or fabricating evidence.

Unless lawyers are protected, it matters little that they are allowed to meet with their clients in the investigation stage rather than immediately before a trial.

Even so, the draft law provides as exception to the right of lawyers to meet with clients who are under detention. It says that in some circumstances, meetings between a lawyer and a detained suspect cannot be held without approval. The exceptions are when the suspected offence "involves a crime endangering state security, a crime of conducting terrorist activities or a major crime of bribery."

Human Rights vs. National Security

In fact, the draft law is replete with exceptions for cases of "endangering state security" [ESS]. And, of course, many human rights lawyers have been accused of doing exactly that.

Current Conditions of Juvenile Criminal Justice in China

China's juvenile criminal justice is in the process of reform and improvement. Statistics show that of all the criminal cases handled by the people's courts in all years, juvenile cases rose from 30,446 in 1997 to 83,697 in 2006, with its proportion in the whole criminal cases rising from 6% in 1997 to 9% in 2006. In order to better adapt to the situation of juvenile criminal cases, China has in recent years accelerated the making of laws concerning juvenile cases. It has adopted two independent laws: the law on the protection of minors (adopted at the 21st session of the Seventh National People's Congress in September 1991) and the law on the prevention of juvenile crimes (adopted at the 10th session of the Ninth National People's Congress in June 1999). This marked a major progress in China's law making.

Jiang Xihui,
"Juvenile Criminal Justice Reform Regarding to Children's Welfare,"
Human Rights Magazine, vol. 10, May 2011.

Much has already been written on the possibility that the new version of the law, originally passed in 1979 and last revised in 1996, would legalize the practice of "disappearing" suspects accused of endangering state security for up to six months, without informing their families.

As the U.S.-based Dui Hua Foundation, which is dedicated to the protection of human rights, has said, "Chinese authorities use ESS crimes in their effort to suppress political dissent in the name of protecting national security."

And the number of such cases has increased dramatically, rising from an average of 289 a year in the 1998–2007 period to 698 cases in 2009 and 670 in 2010.

The ESS exceptions in the draft law reflects its importance as a tool for the Chinese government as it continues its crackdown, including on lawyers who accept human rights cases.

The Juvenile Justice System

On the positive side, Dui Hua hailed the new law's section on juvenile cases and the establishment of a mechanism to exempt certain juvenile criminal suspects from prosecution and incarceration as well as a policy to seal the detention, arrest and incarceration records of most juvenile offenders.

The draft law was posted on the National People's Congress website for public comment for a month on August 30 [2011].

It isn't clear to what extent public views will be taken into consideration before the final draft appears, probably next spring [2012]. The current draft is the result of many years of debate among various groups within the Chinese leadership, with the security authorities playing a major role.

Hopefully, the objectionable provisions will be dropped, or at least modified. But this is probably unlikely.

Indonesia Is on the Verge of Introducing a Restorative Justice System for Juvenile Offenders

Leopold Sudaryono

Leopold Sudaryono is the coordinator of law programs at the Asia Foundation in Indonesia. In the following viewpoint, he reports that a number of controversial legal cases in Indonesia featuring juvenile offenders have spurred a national debate about the state of the nation's juvenile justice system. A new bill pushing for restorative justice, a system that allows offenders to interact and make amends with their victims, has gained traction. Most importantly, the proposed law will raise the age of criminal responsibility. Sudaryono believes that these steps would significantly enhance the legal protections for juvenile offenders in the Indonesian justice system.

As you read, consider the following questions:

1. According to UNICEF, what percentage of children over the age of eight accused of a crime spent somewhere between three months and three years behind bars?

2. How many of Indonesia's juvenile offenders are held in adult detention facilities, according to UNICEF?

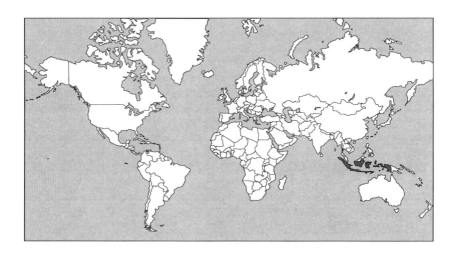

3. What is Indonesia's age of criminal responsibility?

After a series of reports emerged across the archipelago in recent weeks [early 2012] of children being arrested and prosecuted for petty crimes, Indonesians are raising questions about the state of juvenile justice in the country. The first was a confounding case that resonated around the globe: a 15-year-old boy from Central Sulawesi was incarcerated and tried last month [January 2012] after a police officer accused him of stealing a pair of used flip-flops worth about $3. Claims emerged that the boy was badly beaten by police during interrogation, and the officer who reported the minor was formally punished. The case galvanized the Indonesian public, and infuriated citizens collected over a thousand pairs of sandals and dumped them on the steps of police stations across the country.

Days later, news surfaced of a teenager from West Timor who was put on trial for stealing bouquets of flowers from his aunt, and a Balinese teenager who was tried for stealing a wallet containing Rp. 1,000 (around 10 cents). The cases prompted similar outrage and hatched wry campaigns from a frustrated public, with citizens gathering flowers and coins to mock law enforcers for their heavy-handedness.

Sadly, such cases are not uncommon here. If you are a child over the age of eight, are Indonesian or just happen to be in Indonesia, and take someone's property—intentionally or not—and are then reported to the police, there is a high chance you will be prosecuted. According to UNICEF [the United Nations Children's Fund], around 80 percent of children over age eight who were reported to police ended up being tried, with 91 percent of them spending between three months to three years behind bars. Today, there are 5,515 child inmates in Indonesia, 85 percent of whom are in adult detention facilities.

Despite these figures, Indonesian law does offer some protection for children. After ratifying the UN Convention on the Rights of the Child in 1990, Indonesia adopted a special law on juvenile justice in 1997. The law provides for separate court proceedings and some additional post-adjudication stages for children in conflict with the law. But the law contains two major defects, as practitioners and scholars have pointed out.

In most juvenile cases in Indonesia, children are not accompanied by legal counsel, let alone a trained social worker who could minimize harm during the investigation and prosecution process.

Flaws in the System

First, it fails to regulate the pre-adjudication process, when children may be arrested, detained, or have charges pressed against them by the police. In most cases, children—whether guilty or not—are detained in cells alongside adults and interrogated by police who are not properly trained to deal with minors.

Torture or ill treatment to extract information is "routine practice," said UN special rapporteur on torture Manfred

Nowak in his 2008 report on Indonesia, and it is thought to be commonly used by detectives when interrogating minors. In a particularly gruesome recent case, two boys arrested on charges of stealing a mosque collection box and a motorcycle allegedly hanged themselves while in police custody. Their parents claimed the boys' bodies bore clear signs of torture, and the National Human Rights Commission is now reviewing autopsy results.

In most juvenile cases in Indonesia, children are not accompanied by legal counsel, let alone a trained social worker who could minimize harm during the investigation and prosecution process, as well as promote social reintegration instead of incarceration at sentencing.

The law's second major defect is the very low minimum age—eight years—at which children can be formally prosecuted and imprisoned. At these very young ages, crimes tend to be minor—for instance, a recent study by the University of Indonesia's Center on Child Protection found that 53 percent of crimes committed by minors involved petty theft, defined as goods worth less than $12. Children who are incarcerated are at a heightened risk of physical and psychosocial health concerns, in addition to risk of becoming further isolated from society. Despite this, Indonesia's justice system continues to mandate punishment, not rehabilitation.

The problems are not simply a result of poor legislation. A 2002 law on child protection obliges the government and other state institutions to provide special protection to children in conflict with the law. However, since the law does not elaborate on the term "special protection," it has not been effective in binding law enforcement agencies to use the law to promote the best interests of children.

A Renewed Push for Reform

Recognizing the deficiencies in the 1997 law, a new bill on juvenile offenders was submitted last year to parliament, and recent events have sparked a renewed push for its passage. The bill covers all stages of the justice process and uses principles of restorative justice to guide cases involving juveniles from start to finish, including rehabilitation. More importantly, it increases the minimum age at which children can be tried to 12 years old, and would introduce mechanisms to make diversion, or out-of-court solutions, more effective. It is not flawless, but once enacted should significantly increase legal protection for Indonesian children in conflict with the law.

One hopes that revisions to the law can affect real change, but it will likely depend on orchestrated, hard work by agencies across the justice sector that have in the past not coordinated very well. For now, however, police can be sure that the public is watching and is increasingly intolerant of abuses of power by the boys in brown.

Several Nations in Central Asia and Eastern Europe Have Made Major Juvenile Justice System Reforms

Daniel O'Donnell

Daniel O'Donnell is a consultant who collaborates with UNICEF (the United Nations Children's Fund). In the following viewpoint, he reviews recent reforms to the juvenile justice systems in Albania, Azerbaijan, Kazakhstan, Turkey, and the Ukraine. O'Donnell assesses the achievements in areas such as the development of specialized judges, courts, and law enforcement units; the decrease in custodial sentencing; alternative sentencing; and the quality of juvenile correctional facilities. He concludes that although some key reforms and improvements have been made, there are a number of areas that still need work.

As you read, consider the following questions:

1. According to the viewpoint, how many specialized juvenile courts have been created in Kazakhstan?

2. What two countries are planning to build new facilities for juvenile offenders, according to the viewpoint?

Daniel O'Donnell, "The Development of Juvenile Justice Systems in Eastern Europe and Central Asia: Lessons from Albania, Azerbaijan, Kazakhstan, Turkey and Ukraine," July 2009, pp. 16–23. Copyright © 2009 by UNICEF. All rights reserved. Reproduced by permission.

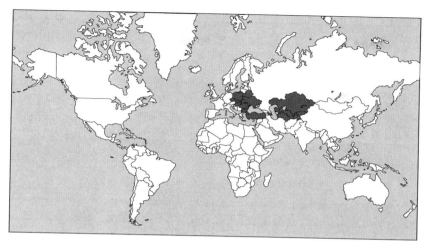

3. What does the author cite as the age of criminal responsibility in Turkey?

In each of the countries covered by the assessment, significant progress has been achieved in the development of juvenile justice systems that meet relevant United Nations and European standards. It is not possible to generalize as to which country or countries have made more progress; in all of them, improvements have been greater in some areas than others and, in each, much remains to be done. The following is an overview of the achievements in different areas of juvenile justice. The boxes identify some of the most positive experiences—including some that could serve as models for other European countries.

The Specialization of Judges and Courts

The appointment of specialized judges or the establishment of specialized courts has been a significant advance in most countries. In Albania, the creation of specialized sections of district courts was envisaged by the Code of Criminal Procedure adopted in 1998, but it was not until 2007 that they were established in six districts. The appointment of specialized judges has improved the quality of juvenile justice, and many expect that specialized sections will be established throughout the country.

Neither juvenile courts nor specialized judges exist in Azerbaijan.

In Kazakhstan, two specialized juvenile courts have been created: one in Almaty and one in Astana. A decree has been adopted recently, calling for the creation of specialized courts throughout the country.

Experience does suggest that specialized juvenile courts are the best solution for most countries.

In Turkey, the first children's court was established in 1988, but it was not until recently that a network of children's courts was expanded significantly. There are now 83 juvenile courts in 25 provinces. They handle cases involving children in need of protection and juveniles accused of an offence. The staff of children's courts includes special workers and psychologists. Specialized prosecutors handle cases assigned to children's courts. These courts have improved the quality of justice, although their heavy caseload has led to excessive delays in the resolution of cases concerning accused juveniles. There are still more than 50 provinces without children's courts, however, and many prosecutors and judges assigned to children's courts have not yet received special training. There are also some important gaps in the competence of children's courts (for example, to determine whether an accused juvenile will be detained prior to trial).

In 2003, the Supreme Court of Ukraine ordered all trial courts to appoint a judge for cases involving juveniles. No special training is required and these judges continue to handle other kinds of cases. Consequently, while some designated judges show sensitivity to the special characteristics of juvenile cases and an understanding of the internationally recognized rights and principles, others do not.

A Complex Issue

The experience of these four countries reveals the complexity of the issue. On one hand, specialized courts or judges devoted exclusively to cases involving juveniles sometimes develop a better understanding of the relevant principles and appropriate methodologies. The extent to which they do so is affected by many variables, including the law they apply, their motivation, recruitment policies, the quality of training, specialization of prosecutors and defence attorneys and the non-judicial staff employed by the courts. Yet some designated judges also develop a good understanding of the relevant principles and appropriate methodologies. In most countries, the number of cases adjudicated does not justify establishing special juvenile courts throughout the entire country, yet giving specialized courts jurisdiction over large territories can cause difficulties for the prosecution and the defence alike. Experience does suggest that specialized juvenile courts are the best solution for most countries, in the cities where the greatest number of cases arise. More generally, one can conclude that the decision as to the establishment of such courts and their location should be based on reliable, disaggregated data on offending, and calculations as to the number of cases that could be handled without trial through diversion mechanisms. No single solution is appropriate for all countries, but it is important for each country facing this issue to learn from the experiences of others.

Specialized Police Units

All five countries covered by the assessment have police units specialized in cases involving children. The extent of their mandate varies considerably: In some countries, for example

Azerbaijan, it is largely limited to preventive activities, while in others it includes children who are suspects or victims of crime.

In Albania, special units of the police were established in 12 prefectures in 2007. They are responsible for cases of domestic violence as well as offending by juveniles.

In Kazakhstan, the mandate of the juvenile police has expanded to include the investigation of offending by juveniles. They continue to play a central role in prevention, and their approach to prevention has evolved to include a police presence in schools.

The creation of special police forces for children and adolescents helps prevent violations of children's rights by law enforcement officials and protects children who are victims of crimes.

In Turkey, a special unit of the national police responsible for child victims was established in 1997. In 2001, its mandate was expanded to include offending by juveniles. The Children's Police have 3,500 officers and staff and is present throughout the country. They have a record of good treatment of children and are gradually helping to change the culture of the police force as a whole towards greater respect for the rights of children, whether victims or suspects. This, too, can be considered a model for other countries.

In Ukraine, the juvenile police now have responsibility for children victims of crime as well as juvenile offenders. They also operate 'reception/distribution' centres, which have a broad range of functions, including temporary detention or shelter for runaways, juveniles suspected of offending and illegal migrants under age 18. One such centre visited by the assessment team can be considered a model.

The creation of special police forces for children and adolescents helps prevent violations of children's rights by law enforcement officials and protects children who are victims of crimes. The broader their role is, in particular in investigating offences, the more value they bring to a juvenile justice system, but the creation of such specialized units does not obviate the need for effective monitoring of the interaction of other police units with children and adolescents. Their effectiveness in preventing offending by children is unclear, but it is obvious that they should not have primary responsibility for prevention and, especially, they should not be given a dominant role in administrative decisions that may deprive children of their liberty.

The Decrease in Custodial Sentences

In all countries covered by the assessment there has been a decrease in the number or percentage of convicted juveniles given custodial sentences and in the number of juvenile prisoners. In Azerbaijan, the percentage of convicted offenders receiving 'conditional' or suspended sentences increased substantially in 2001, from below 30 per cent to around 50 per cent. In Kazakhstan, data on sentencing indicate that the percentage of convicted juveniles given 'suspended' sentences rose from 11 per cent in 1996 to 65 per cent in 2000. In Turkey, the number of juveniles sentenced to juvenile correctional facilities fell sharply from 706 in 1998 to 78 in 2006. (This has been unfortunately tarnished by the high number of children recently sentenced under the antiterrorist laws.) In Ukraine, the total population of correctional facilities has fallen by roughly one-half during the last decade [from 1999 to 2009].

The decrease in the use of custodial sentences documented in most of these countries, which appears to be the main reason for the decline in the number of juvenile prisoners, may be attributed in part to changes in the applicable legislation, and in part to a drop in offending. The main reason appears to be the training of judges and, to a lesser extent, of prosecutors. The reduced use of custodial sentences is an indicator of greater respect for the internationally recognized principle that deprivation of liberty shall be the 'last resort'.

While the use of custodial sentences is declining, resorting to detention during investigation and trial remains a serious problem. In Albania, for example, 40 per cent of all accused juveniles are detained prior to trial and, at the time of the assessment mission, 82 per cent of all juveniles deprived of liberty were in detention facilities. In Turkey, 90 per cent of all juveniles deprived of liberty are in pretrial detention centres, not correctional facilities for convicted juveniles.

Improved Conditions in Juvenile Correctional Facilities

Conditions in correctional facilities for convicted juvenile offenders have improved in all five countries covered by the assessment. Overcrowding was not detected in any of the facilities visited; indeed, the population of most is well under capacity.

In most countries there have been no major improvements in the physical infrastructure of prisons and detention facilities, although the construction of new facilities for juvenile offenders is planned in Albania and Azerbaijan. The improvements concern the kind of programmes, activities and services provided, staff's attitudes towards prisoners as well as visitation policies and discipline methods.

Evaluating conditions in correctional facilities is, of course, difficult. The assessment team did not interview prisoners and, with one exception, available studies or reports including interviews with juvenile prisoners were not recent enough to ascertain whether the description of current conditions was reliable. Consequently, the following conclusions are based mainly on interviews with facilities' staff and independent sources knowledgeable about conditions.

One advance observed in all five countries is the addition of psychologists and social workers to the staff. Although this is a very positive development, in some countries there are problems that remain to be solved, such as the difficulty in recruiting experienced and qualified psychologists due to unattractive salaries, frequent absenteeism, and nonrecognition of the confidentiality of the relationship between prisoners and psychologists by the staff of the correctional facilities.

The process of developing legislation on juvenile justice in harmony with international standards is still under way.

Other achievements include access to standard and remedial education; clean living areas with amenities such as windows, refrigerators and cabinets for personal effects; adequate food, clothing, bedding and medical care; generous access to recreational activities, especially sports; efforts to encourage and facilitate contact between prisoners and their families; respect for religious practices (e.g., prayer rooms, special meals during fasting) and access to religious counsellors; and participation in cultural activities, such as art, music, theatre, literature and chess. Vocational training is provided in order to enable prisoners to find employment after release. Forced labour was not detected in any of the correctional facilities visited.

The facilities visited take a preventive approach to disciplinary problems and strive to resolve regulation infractions through warnings or counselling, when possible. The use of corporal punishment is banished, although there is conflicting information on how well this prohibition is enforced in some of the facilities visited. Regulations permitting sanctions that are not allowed by international standards, such as confinement in isolation cells or suspension of the right to receive or make family visits, are still in force in most of the countries visited.

Basic Economic and Demographic Indicators in Albania, Azerbaijan, Kazakhstan, Turkey, and Ukraine			
	GNI per capita	Total population	Under-18 population
Albania	US$ 3,290	3.19 million	31%
Azerbaijan	US$ 2,550	8.46 million	30%
Kazakhstan	US$ 5,060	15.42 million	29%
Turkey	US$ 8,020	74.87 million	33%
Ukraine	US$ 2,550	46.2 million	18%

These data come from the UNICEF report *The State of the World's Children 2009*.

TAKEN FROM: Daniel O'Donnell, "The Development of Juvenile Justice Systems in Eastern Europe and Central Asia: Lessons from Albania, Azerbaijan, Kazakhstan, Turkey and Ukraine," UNICEF, July 2009.

Some Limited but Positive Elements of Law Reform

The process of developing legislation on juvenile justice in harmony with international standards is still under way. There are plans to adopt new legislation in Albania, Azerbaijan, Kazakhstan and Ukraine, and further reforms are needed in Turkey. Yet in all of these countries, some important changes in the law have already been made: children may not be interrogated without the presence of a lawyer and/or psychologist; and the right of accused juveniles to legal assistance is recognized.

In Albania, legislation adopted during the 1990s recognizes the right of juveniles not to be detained with adults.

In Kazakhstan, legislation adopted in 1997 requires pre-sentence reports and recognizes alternative sentences. If a juvenile suspect is detained, charges must be filed within 72 hours. Juvenile suspects may not be interrogated for more than two hours at a time, nor at night.

In Turkey, recent legislation raised the minimum age for the prosecution of juvenile offenders to age 12, and an amendment to older legislation gave juvenile courts competence over offenders aged 15–18 years. The use of handcuffs on juveniles is prohibited; children under age 15 may not be detained prior to trial unless charged with a serious offence; and juveniles in detention have the right to be accompanied by a relative.

In Ukraine, juvenile suspects may not be interrogated alone or for more than two hours at a time and they may not be detained before trial unless accused of a serious offence; the maximum sentence that may be imposed on convicted juveniles was reduced to 10 years.

Length of Detention

The duration of proceedings is an area where the need to amend legislation is urgent. Legislation adopted in recent years invariably recognizes the right of accused juveniles to be tried 'without delay', but in most countries specific time limits do not adequately protect this principle and are often the same for juveniles and adults.

The Committee on the Rights of the Child recommends that children deprived of their liberty should be presented to a judge within 24 hours. Police may detain juvenile suspects for 48 hours without a court order in Albania; for 24 or 48 hours, depending on the circumstances, in Azerbaijan; for up to 72 hours in Kazakhstan; and, in Turkey, a juvenile suspected of committing offences jointly with another person may be detained for up to four days.

The Committee on the Rights of the Child recommends that children should not be detained for purposes of investigation without charges for more than 30 days. In Azerbaijan, the time limit for completing the entire investigation is, in principle, two to four months, and detention prior to trial should normally not exceed three months.

The Committee on the Rights of the Child recommends that, once charges have been placed, the trial should be concluded within six months. In Albania, the maximum duration of detention prior to trial is three years, for juveniles and adults alike. The law fixes no time limits on the duration of investigation and trial if the suspect/accused is not deprived of liberty. In Kazakhstan, the time limit for trials of juveniles is one year. In Turkey, it normally is one year if the accused is detained, but may be up to three years for some offences. In Ukraine, the law does not set a time limit to the duration of detention prior to and during trial.

There is clearly a need for the process of law reform to continue in all five countries.

The Timid Emergence of Diversion

Diversion may take the form of a simple warning, but it often takes the form of mediation, compensation of the victim or voluntary participation in some kind of prevention/rehabilitation programme. Diversion is a relatively recent development in civil law countries. Some progress has been achieved concerning its recognition in the countries covered by this assessment, and some pilot projects include programmes for offenders whose cases are diverted. In general, where the law recognizes diversion it does so only in narrow circumstances, and some pilot diversion projects operate with a tenuous legal basis.

In Albania, an interesting pilot project is operating in four districts. Cases involving minor injuries or insults can be referred for mediation, and if the victim is compensated the case is closed.

In Azerbaijan, the investigation of a crime may be discontinued, the prosecutor may decide not to proceed to trial, or the court may decide to discontinue proceedings in the following circumstances: the accused is a first offender; he/she shows remorse; he/she has pled guilty; he/she has reconciled with and compensated the victim; and he/she no longer represents a serious danger to society.

A Pilot Programme

A pilot diversion project for juveniles was established in the capital in 2007. It does not rely on the procedure described above, but rather on the referral of cases to the Commission on Minors, an administrative body having broad competence over cases involving antisocial behaviour and minor offences. Most of the cases referred to this project involve antisocial behaviour, not offending. The cases that do involve offending are referred by a local court as 'alternative sentencing'. It is not clear whether the project actually provides diversion. It could be considered secondary prevention. It includes remedial education, life skills training, counselling and other forms of assistance. The project's impact on beneficiaries and on offending has not yet been evaluated.

In Kazakhstan, cases involving offences of minor or average seriousness may be closed without proceeding to trial if the victim and the offender have reconciled and the victim has been compensated. A pilot project implemented in Astana facilitated mediation for this purpose. Although the police still practise this form of diversion, it has not been promoted on the national level.

In Turkey, prosecutors have discretion not to prosecute if the accused is a first offender and the crime is not a serious one. Other conditions are: compensation of the victim, if appropriate and possible; a finding that the offender is unlikely to commit another offence; and a finding that deferral of proceedings is in the interest of society. If these conditions are met, the judge may decide to postpone trial for five years and, if no offence is committed during this period, the case is closed.

Trial also may be avoided if a juvenile offender compensates the victim through a procedure known as 'negotiating and settling'. This form of diversion is available only for minor crimes, but there is no requirement that the juvenile be a first offender. When first recognized, trained mediators participated in the procedure, but after a short period their role was eliminated, because authorities attribute more importance to compensation than to reconciliation.

In Ukraine, a prosecutor can recommend that the court impose 'compulsory measures of an educational nature' in certain circumstances, if both the accused child and his/her parents agree. The measures include warnings, restrictions on behaviour and supervision or placement in a special educational and correctional institution. Such a recommendation can be made only if the prosecutor concludes that a juvenile first offender who has committed a minor offence or a crime of moderate severity can be rehabilitated without criminal sanction, or if he/she concludes that the juvenile did not fully understand the nature or consequences of his/her behaviour. A pilot project involving victim-offender mediation (VOM) began in 2007 in two regions. The Ministry of Justice has prepared a draft law on VOM.

The fact that some form of diversion now exists in each of the five countries is an accomplishment, although much remains to be done in terms of adopting legislation, broadening the range of cases in which diversion is available, and taking to scale VOM and other community-based programmes that provide appropriate prevention/rehabilitation services on a voluntary basis as a means of avoiding unnecessary legal proceedings.

Alternative Sentences and Reforms

The term 'alternative sentences' is usually used as a synonym for sentences that do not involve deprivation of liberty, such as warnings; fines; compensation of the victim; probation and other forms of supervision; orders concerning behaviour; mandatory participation in counselling or other programmes designed to prevent re-offending; and community service. The term is sometimes used more broadly to include sentences where the offender is deprived of liberty on a part-time basis (e.g., on weekends or at night). Sentences to an open correctional facility are not considered as alternative sentences, however. Alternative sentences are important as a means of compliance with the principle that no child shall be deprived of liberty except as a 'last resort', as required by article 37(b) of the Convention on the Rights of the Child.

All legal systems have some non-custodial sentences. Warnings and supervision were widely used under the Soviet legal system. Supervision was done by the police. Confinement in psychiatric hospitals and substance abuse centres were used as well. In some countries, other non-custodial sentences were recognized by law, but the programmes or services needed to put them into practice did not exist.

The kind of alternative sentences available has expanded in most of the countries covered by the assessment. Some of them are implementing pilot projects offering new programmes and services. In Albania, sentences to community service have been recognized by law since 1995, but there were no programmes to supervise such orders until UNICEF [the United Nations Children's Fund] took the initiative of supporting a pilot project in 2007. Similarly, the law recognized probation, but no probation service existed. A law authorizing the establishment of probation was adopted in 2008.

In Azerbaijan, the alternative sentence most commonly imposed on juveniles is the 'conditional' sentence, which is similar to probation. The number of conditional sentences, fines and community service sentences imposed on juveniles has increased dramatically. There are, however, no community-based programmes designed to assist juveniles given non-custodial sentences.

In Kazakhstan, judges may impose warning, release in the custody of parents, reparation of the damage, restrictions or requirements regarding the offender's conduct if they conclude that confinement in a correctional facility is not necessary for the rehabilitation of a juvenile convicted of a minor offence or a first offender aged 16–18 years convicted of offences of average gravity. Judges also have broader discretion to impose a conditional sentence if they conclude that confinement in a correctional facility is not necessary to prevent re-offending. More than half of all sentences imposed on juvenile offenders are conditional, and the number of non-custodial sentences has increased substantially, which seems to indicate growing judicial sensitivity to the 'best interests of the child' and the 'last resort' principles.

Using Discretion in Sentencing

In Turkey, sentences of less than one year must be converted into non-custodial sentences, which include fines, community service, restrictions on activities and freedom of movement, and enrollment in an educational institution. Judges have discretion to suspend sentences of three years or less for a first offender, if he/she has expressed remorse and the judge concludes that he/she is unlikely to re-offend. If the offender is under age 15, this discretion extends to sentences of up to five years. Sentencing may be avoided through reconciliation between the victim and the offender.

In Ukraine, first offenders may not be given a custodial sentence for a minor offence, and judges have discretion to impose an alternative sentence if they conclude that confinement in a correctional facility is not needed to prevent re-offending. Judges also have discretion to simply dismiss charges related to a minor or medium-gravity offence if the offender has demonstrated repentance and irreproachable conduct—a good example of legislation that facilitates compliance with the 'last resort' principle. Juvenile offenders sentenced to a term of five years or less may benefit from probation. An agency is responsible for supervising offenders given this sentence.

While considerable progress has been made in introducing alternative sentences, in particular those that involve the provision of assistance to avoid re-offending, this process remains in an early stage. It is important to evaluate the impact of pilot projects and new legislation, especially on re-offending and, in most countries, to gradually expand the programmes available for offenders given non-custodial sentences. Research also is needed on the risk of re-offending for different kinds of crimes and the circumstances in which they are committed, with a view to re-evaluating the basis for restrictions on the discretion of judges to apply alternative sentences.

Ukraine Is Creating a Full-Fledged Youth Justice System

Vyacheslav Panasyuk

Vyacheslav Panasyuk is head of the division of justice of the Ministry of Justice of Ukraine. In the following viewpoint, he commends the introduction of the Concept for Development of Criminal Justice for Minors in Ukraine, which outlines the new approach the state is taking to address the problem of juvenile crime. Key to the concept are plans for a restorative justice system for young offenders and an improved approach to rehabilitation. Panasyuk notes that the implementation of the concept means a full-fledged juvenile justice system in the Ukraine, one that ensures the protection of children.

As you read, consider the following questions:

1. According to Panasyuk, how many minors were incarcerated in Ukraine's youth colonies as of January 2011?

2. How effective is restorative justice, according to about ten years of experience using such approaches in Ukraine?

3. Over what time period does Panasyuk suggest that the concept should be implemented?

Vyacheslav Panasyuk, "Criminal Justice for Minors Is a Civilized Approach by the State to Dealing with the Problem of Youth Criminality," Ukraine Juvenile Justice Reform Project, Newsletter #3, September 2011, pp. 2–4. Reproduced by permission.

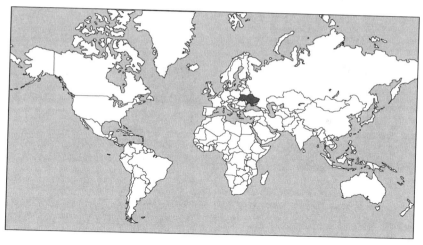

On May 24, 2011, the president of Ukraine signed Decree #597 introducing a Concept [for] Development of Criminal Justice for Minors in Ukraine.

This concept was developed by a working group which was formed by an order of the Ministry of Justice, dated 27 May 2010, ref. #491/7. The working group was comprised of representatives of the Supreme Court of Ukraine, central bodies of the executive authority, the general prosecutor's office, the Institute for Legislation under the Supreme Council, the correctional system and nongovernmental organizations.

It should be noted that the final version of the concept included work that had been developed by another working group formed earlier under the auspices of the Supreme Court of Ukraine and which also included representatives of state bodies as well as members of the public.

What Is the Concept?

The provisions of the concept demonstrate that the state is undertaking a new approach to the problem of youth criminality and protection of children's rights, considering that children are a special category of persons in any society. Due to their social and developmental immaturity, young people are not capable of fully realizing the nature of their actions nor are they able to anticipate the full range of negative consequences those actions might have on themselves or others. At the same time, they are future full-fledged members of the society and, in essence, they are another link in society's continued existence. On the part of the state, rule of law and social justice can only be achieved if the state creates proper conditions for every child for the full and harmonious development of her or his personality. For that reason, it is necessary to consider a young person's age, social and psychological factors and other specifics of their development in dealing with youth issues.

The Constitution of Ukraine recognizes the life and health of individuals and their honour and dignity as the highest of social values.

There are a significant number of international documents whose provisions are aimed at the protection of children's rights, including, in particular:

1. United Nations Convention on the Rights of the Child, 1989;

2. United Nations Guidelines for the Prevention of Juvenile Delinquency and United Nations Rules for the Protection of Juveniles Deprived of Their Liberty, 1990;

3. Recommendation of the Committee of Ministers of the Council [of] Europe to member states concerning new ways of dealing with juvenile delinquency and the role of juvenile justice, 2003;

4. Recommendation of the Committee of Ministers of the Council [of] Europe to member states on social reactions to juvenile delinquency, 1987;

5. Recommendation of the Committee of Ministers of the Council of Europe to member states on the role of early psychosocial intervention in the prevention of criminality, 2000;

6. The European Convention on the Exercise of Children's Rights, 1996.

These and other documents indicate that the issue at hand requires the special attention on the part of any state.

The Constitution of Ukraine recognizes the life and health of individuals and their honour and dignity as the highest of social values. Every person has the right to the free development of their personality. Children are equal in their rights regardless of their origin, or whether they were born within or outside of a marriage. The rights and freedoms of individuals and their respective guarantees define the content and direction of development of the state.

Ukraine Legislation Regarding Children

Depending on the area of regulation of social relations, Ukrainian legislation contains a number of specifics that concern legal relationships with children.

The Civil Code of Ukraine recognizes that individuals may have partial civil capacity and incomplete civil capacity, depending on the age of the party to a legal relationship. In particular, small children and underage persons are considered to have partial civil capacity and incomplete civil capacity, which affects their civil responsibilities.

In the same way, the Criminal Code of Ukraine also defines criminal accountability by age and establishes a number of specifics regarding criminal liability and punishment of minors.

In addition, the Criminal Procedure Code of Ukraine lays out special provisions regarding the proceedings of cases involving minors. In particular, it defines the exceptional cases in which a minor can be detained or taken into custody, outlines the procedure for applying enforcement measures of an educational nature, and provides for the possibility to close a criminal case in the event that an offence committed by a minor is of small or medium gravity. The Criminal Procedure Code also provides a list of circumstances which should be defined during the pretrial phase including personal characteristics of minors; their living and upbringing conditions; circumstances that negatively influenced their upbringing; existence or absence of adult instigators and other persons who involved the minor in criminal activity.

Absence of consistency and lack of coordination between agencies that deal with young people also lead to problems in law enforcement.

Needed Improvements

The above shows that significant attention is given to the observance of children's rights in Ukraine, which corresponds to most widely recognized international standards. At the same time, it should be noted that a number of provisions in the current legislation require significant updating to meet today's requirements, considering developments in legal thought around juvenile justice. Likewise, there is a necessity to implement new methods of working with young offenders.

Imperfections in legislation inevitably create problems in the area of enforcement of law, making it impossible for those who are involved in the system (including judges, on whose decisions the further fate of young offenders depends) to exercise their authority to its full extent in terms of administering independent, objective and unbiased justice.

Absence of consistency and lack of coordination between agencies that deal with young people also lead to problems in law enforcement. Most importantly, a lack of agency coordination means that it is difficult to develop coordinated and proven approaches to working with young offenders. This is particularly true, for example, with regard to the procedure for submitting documents to the court that assess the needs and re-offending risk of the young person, and the procedure for providing legal support to such a person in the process of the administration of justice, etc.

As a result, the measures taken do not improve young offenders' unlawful behaviour and the situation concerning the level of youth criminality and its recurrence, with the result that such circumstances neutralize the effect of the very essence of an imposed measure.

It should be noted that as of January 2011, 1,432 minors are incarcerated in Ukraine's youth colonies. More than half of them (54.8%) were sentenced to deprivation of liberty (i.e., custody) for a term of three to five years; 58.3% of them were held criminally accountable in the past and their punishment did not involve deprivation of liberty; 24.9% of the minors did not study or work prior to their conviction. Obviously, such a situation is not acceptable and it is not in line with the direction of development that the state of Ukraine has chosen.

A More Effective Juvenile Justice System

Considering the aforementioned, it has become necessary today to undertake a quality review and revision of current legislation in the area of criminal justice for minors to promote more effective cooperation between agencies and services dealing with minors, and facilitate the involvement of communities and civil society institutions into the social reintegration of young offenders. First and foremost, such steps need to be taken for the purpose of ensuring the correctness and effectiveness of every legal decision made in regard to a child who has come into conflict with the law, while at the same time ensuring that such decisions are aimed at their reeducation and further social support.

Some Positive Developments in the Ukraine's Juvenile Justice System

• Some important institutional reforms have taken place: specialized juvenile police units have been established throughout the country, and all trial courts have judges designated to handle cases involving juvenile offenders.

• Data concerning offending by juveniles and juvenile justice reveal some very positive trends: the number of offences by juveniles has fallen by one-half since 2000; the population of correctional colonies for juvenile offenders has decreased by one-third since 2003; and facilities for underage offenders are at 20 per cent of their capacity...

• Valuable research on the treatment of accused and convicted juvenile offenders has taken place, with the full cooperation of relevant authorities. The State Statistics Committee is attempting to coordinate and harmonize sectoral data collection mechanisms in order to create a common database, which can provide evidence that will help inform policy making, law reform and planning.

• The president of Ukraine recently made a commitment to develop a comprehensive juvenile justice system, and most agencies and institutions concerned with juvenile justice seem willing, if not eager, to get on with this task. In general, there appears to be a commitment to compliance with international standards and interest in learning from other countries' experience.

TAKEN FROM: Daniel O'Donnell, "Assessment of Juvenile Justice Reform Achievements in Ukraine," UNICEF, July 2009.

The concept defines the main directions for developing a criminal justice system for minors in Ukraine, which are intended to enhance the responsibility of the family, community and the state in the process of the upbringing and development of children; to uphold the rights and freedoms of children who have come into conflict with the law by raising the level of their legal and social protection; and to decrease the level of youth criminality and its recurrence.

In order to achieve the goal defined by the concept, a number of measures are to be defined, aiming to improve the system of prevention of youth criminality and provide effective justice for minors who have committed offences or other violations of law. These measures will focus, in particular, on the development of restorative justice and on creating an effective system of rehabilitation of minors who have committed violations of law in order to ensure their reeducation and resocialization.

Thus far in Ukraine, mechanisms of restorative justice and the mediation procedure (reconciliation) have been applied only within the framework of pilot projects.

In regard to prevention in particular, the following is planned: to carry out information and explanatory work with families; to introduce up-to-date methods and forms of working with children who are inclined to commit violations of law; to improve monitoring of the youth criminality situation and observance of the rights of children who have come into conflict with the law; etc.

Restorative Justice

Justice for minors has to be administered with considerations of age, sociopsychological, psychophysical and other specifics of their development and this has to be done, in particular, through the training of judges, public prosecutors, lawyers, employees of agencies and services related to minors' affairs in terms of administration of judicial proceedings; providing minors with access to free legal support; facilitating the development of restorative justice, in particular through the introduction of mediation procedures as an effective means for voluntary reconciliation between the victim and the offender;

helping shape young offenders' sense of responsibility for their actions and encouraging them to accept responsibility for remedying the inflicted harm and bringing about positive changes in their behaviour; and involving the community into the resolution of a conflict in case there is active participation of the parties in the process of restoration of damaged relationships.

In this regard, it should be noted that, currently, mechanisms of restorative justice have been effective in many developed countries for many years, and their application demonstrates a high level of effectiveness. Thus far in Ukraine, mechanisms of restorative justice and the mediation procedure (reconciliation) have been applied only within the framework of pilot projects. However, about 10 years of experience in using such approaches demonstrate effective results in 90 percent of cases: It is possible to achieve real changes in the behaviour of a young offender without imposing a punishment that involves incarceration, for the offender to provide the victim with real compensation for the damage inflicted due to an offence, and for the victim and the offender to reconcile with each other, as well as to eliminate the risk of the minor's re-offending.

Various Rehabilitation Programs

Coming back to the concept, it should be noted that an effective system of rehabilitation of minors who have committed offences has to be created. The purposes of such a system are to reeducate and resocialize young people through the development and application of corresponding correctional, educational-informational and psychological-pedagogical programs. To support this goal, it is proposed to create a juvenile probation service that would be responsible for supervising young offenders and their social adaptation and reintegration, and in assisting them with rebuilding their lives by supporting their efforts regarding education and employment.

The concept should be implemented over the period of the next five years. For this purpose, the above-mentioned decree of the president of Ukraine instructed the cabinet of ministers of Ukraine to develop and approve, within a three-month period, an action plan to implement the provisions of the concept. The plan will contain specific tasks, designate state bodies to implement the tasks and will establish time periods for its fulfillment.

Developing a Juvenile Justice System

Implementation of the concept will result in the creation of a full-fledged juvenile justice system in Ukraine, ensuring proper and effective legal decisions with regard to children who have come into conflict with the law, ensuring that court decisions are focused on the reeducation and further social support of young offenders, and with the goal of decreasing the level of youth criminality and its recurrence.

Along with that, taking into account that provisions of the concept are ideological in nature and the concept itself is, in essence, a legal guideline for further development, it would be an achievement in itself if the implementation of the concept improves public understanding of the importance and need to protect the rights and interests of children as a prerequisite for further embodiment of the above-declared ideas for the good of future generations.

Periodical and Internet Sources Bibliography

The following articles have been selected to supplement the diverse views presented in this chapter.

Rayeesa Absal	"Reforming Young Minds for a Fresh Start in Life," *Gulf News* (Dubai), August 16, 2010.
Sana Altaf	"Juveniles Get No Justice in Kashmir," Inter Press Service, July 29, 2011. www.ipsnews.net.
Pamela Cox	"Juvenile Justice Reform and Policy Convergence in the New Vietnam," *Youth Justice*, vol. 10, no. 3, December 2010.
Joseph Elunya	"Uganda: Alternative Justice for Juvenile Offenders," Radio Netherlands Worldwide, March 23, 2012.
Gulf News (Dubai)	"Children's Courts to Be Set Up in Delhi," January 1, 2011.
Alexsei Kuznetzov	"Sorry, Kids: Russia Says 'Be Home by 10,'" CBS News, June 1, 2009.
Los Angeles Times	"In California, Justice for Juveniles," March 27, 2012.
Alice Miles	"Locking Up Children Is Criminal," *New Statesman*, September 20, 2010.
Anna Mehler Paperny	"Canada's Youth Crime Plans Bewilder International Observers," *Globe and Mail* (Canada), July 19, 2011.
Mark Sherman	"Court Wary of Life Without Parole for Juveniles," *Huffington Post*, March 20, 2012. www.huffingtonpost.com.

For Further Discussion

Chapter 1

1. This chapter examines how various countries treat juvenile crime. After comparing these strategies, identify the approach you feel is most promising. Why?
2. Youth gang crime is a concern in a number of different countries. Is it a problem where you live? What strategies does your community employ to address it?
3. Do American schools criminalize unruly behavior? Read the viewpoint by Chris McGreal to inform your answer.

Chapter 2

1. What are some of the risk factors that cause juvenile crime as mentioned in the viewpoints in this chapter? Which do you feel are present in your community?

Chapter 3

1. One of the major debates in several countries is the age of responsibility of juvenile offenders. At what age do you believe that juveniles should be held criminally responsible for their actions? Justify your answer.
2. Should juvenile offenders be incarcerated in adult institutions? Read the viewpoints in the chapter to inform your opinion.

Chapter 4

1. In the viewpoints in this chapter, it is clear that several countries are debating two very different approaches to juvenile crime: tougher laws, which favor higher rates of incarceration, or more lenient laws, which lean toward

rehabilitation and social welfare programs. Which approach do you favor, and why?

2. The restorative justice movement has gained favor in some countries in recent years. It is even used in some communities and correctional institutions in the United States. What is your opinion on the process of restorative justice? How would it benefit your community?

Organizations to Contact

The editors have compiled the following list of organizations concerned with the issues debated in this book. The descriptions are derived from materials provided by the organizations. All have publications or information available for interested readers. The list was compiled on the date of publication of the present volume; the information provided here may change. Be aware that many organizations take several weeks or longer to respond to inquiries, so allow as much time as possible.

Annie E. Casey Foundation

701 St. Paul Street, Baltimore, MD   21202
(410) 547-6600 • fax: (410) 547-6624
e-mail: webmail@aecf.org
website: www.aecf.org

The Annie E. Casey Foundation is a private charitable organization that is dedicated to supporting public policies that help at-risk children in the United States. The foundation funds grants to help states and communities foster innovative and cost-effective strategies to address juvenile delinquency. One of the organization's key projects is Juvenile Detention Alternatives Initiative (JDAI), which "seeks to help youth involved in the juvenile justice system develop into healthy, productive adults through policies and programs that maximize their chance for success, reduce their likelihood of incarceration, and minimize the risk they pose to their communities." The foundation has also crafted initiatives that develop leaders, strengthen families, and reform child welfare systems in many communities. The foundation website provides a range of information and statistics on child welfare in the Kids Count Data Center.

Campaign for Youth Justice (CFYJ)

1012 Fourteenth Street NW, Suite 610
Washington, DC   20005

(202) 558-3580 • fax: (202) 386-9807
e-mail: info@cfyj.org
website: www.campaignforyouthjustice.org

The Campaign for Youth Justice (CFYJ) is an American organization that works to abolish the controversial criminal justice policy of trying, sentencing, and incarcerating youth under the age of eighteen in the adult criminal justice system. CFYJ believes that placing juveniles in an adult system is a travesty of justice because it puts thousands of young people at risk for often minor infractions. CFYJ advocates reforms of current policies and advances a number of alternative approaches to youth justice that are more fair and effective. The organization's website features breaking news, press releases, news archives, relevant articles, links to radio and television appearances, and a blog that touches on matters of interest. There are a number of other resources available on the CFYJ website.

Canadian Institute for the Administration of Justice (CIAJ)

Faculty of Law, University of Montreal
Pavilion Maximilien-Caron, 3101 Chemin de la Tour
Room A-3421, PO Box 6128, Station Centre Ville
Montreal, Quebec   H3C 3J7
   Canada
(514) 343-6157 • fax: (514) 343-6296
e-mail: ciaj@ciaj-icaj.ca
website: www.ciaj-icaj.ca

The Canadian Institute for the Administration of Justice (CIAJ) is a nonprofit organization that works to improve the quality of justice for all Canadians, including juveniles. CIAJ collaborates with national, provincial, and local governments; professional associations; law schools; attorneys; and the public to support fair and effective criminal justice policies for youth offenders. To that end, the CIAJ organizes conferences and seminars focused on criminal justice reform, administrative and regulatory law and practice, and issues relevant to the

Canadian juvenile justice system. It also sponsors the publications of policy papers and briefs, as well as publishes a newsletter, which is available to members on the CIAJ website.

Coalition for Juvenile Justice (CJJ)

1319 F Street NW, Suite 402, Washington, DC   20004
(202) 467-0864 • fax: (202) 887-0738
e-mail: info@juvjustice.org
website: www.juvjustice.org

The Coalition for Juvenile Justice (CJJ) is "a nationwide coalition of State Advisory Groups (SAGs) and allies dedicated to preventing children and youth from becoming involved in the courts and upholding the highest standards of care when youth are charged with wrongdoing and enter the justice system." CJJ focuses on promoting sound policies regarding preventing and addressing juvenile delinquency; educating the public on criminal justice policy; advocating reforms to improve racial/ethnic disparities in juvenile justice; and facilitating cooperation between national, state, and local officials to improve the juvenile justice system. The CJJ website provides access to the organization's publications on a range of juvenile justice concerns, including policy and legal briefs. *Juvenile Justice e-Monitor*, a monthly e-newsletter, is also available online.

Defence for Children International (DCI)

1, rue de Varembé, PO Box 88, Geneva 20   CH 1211
   Switzerland
+41 0 22 734 05 58 • fax: +41 0 22 740 11 45
e-mail: info@dci-is.org
website: www.defenceforchildren.org

Defence for Children International (DCI) is an independent, nongovernmental organization that strives to protect children's rights all over the world. One of DCI's major objectives is to advocate for fair and effective juvenile justice policies and to stand up for the rights of young people who come in conflict with the law. DCI works "with police officers, judges, and other professionals to train them in guaranteeing the rights of

children in juvenile justice systems." The organization publishes the *DCI Newsletter*, a quarterly update on DCI events
and initiatives, and the *Juvenile Justice Newsletter*, which examines topics of interest in the field. Both are available on the
DCI website. Also available are testimonials, fact sheets, reports, brochures, press releases, and information on upcoming
events.

European Youth Forum
Rue Joseph II Straat 120, Brussels   B-1000
  Belgium
+32 2 230 64 90 • fax: +32 2 230 21 23
website: www.youthforum.org

The European Youth Forum is an international organization
established in 1996 to bring together national youth councils
and international nongovernmental youth organizations across
Europe to advocate for juvenile rights. Its key aims are increasing youth participation in public policy and society; promoting the exchange of ideas among young European people;
and developing and supporting fair and sound policies for
youth, especially in the realm of juvenile justice. The
organization's website features *e-Youth Opinion*, an e-newsletter
covering topics of interest, and *Youth Policy Watch*, a biweekly
bulletin that examines the latest news in the field.

Global Youth Justice (GYJ)
19 Henderson Street, Somerville, MA   02145
(202) 468-3790
e-mail: questions@globalyouthjustice.org
website: www.globalyouthjustice.org

Global Youth Justice (GYJ) was formed to reduce juvenile incarceration rates and address the problem of juvenile crime
around the world "by advancing the global expansion of quality youth justice and juvenile justice diversion programs commonly referred to as youth court, teen court, peer court, student court, youth peer jury, and youth peer panel." By globally
expanding the use of youth courts and harnessing the power

of peer pressure, GYJ also hopes to empower youths and develop leadership in the area of crime prevention, conflict mediation, rehabilitation, and the criminal justice system. There are a range of materials, including statistics, training manuals, and guidebooks, available on the Global Youth Justice website. There is also a link to the GYJ YouTube channel, which offers several short films on the efficacy of youth courts and GYJ programs around the world.

Interagency Panel on Juvenile Justice (IPJJ)

1, rue de Varembé, PO Box 88, Geneva 20 CH 1211
   Switzerland
+41 0 22 734 05 58 • fax: +41 0 22 740 11 45
e-mail: contact@ipjj.org
website: www.ipjj.org

The Interagency Panel on Juvenile Justice (IPJJ) was established by the United Nations in 2000 to provide technical assistance in the area of juvenile justice and to help member states comply with international standards on the treatment of juvenile offenders. The IPJJ is made up of twelve United Nations agencies and nongovernmental organizations that focus on juvenile justice matters. These groups "encourage governments to adopt comprehensive juvenile justice reform programmes and to set clear reform policy targets" regarding children's liberties. The IPJJ's recommendations to certain governments are included in reports accessible on the panel's website. Also available online are breaking news, updates on recent initiatives and activities, and other resources on juvenile justice around the world.

International Juvenile Justice Observatory (IJJO)

Rue Mercelis, No. 50, Brussels 1050
   Belgium
+00 32 262 988 90 • fax: +00 32 262 988 99
e-mail: ijjo@ijjo.org
website: http://ijjo.org

The International Juvenile Justice Observatory (IJJO) is a foundation that brings together professional associations, legislators and policy makers, political groups, social service organizations, and nongovernmental organizations to develop an international forum to exchange information on research, practices, proposals, and initiatives in the juvenile justice field. The IJJO facilitates a network of knowledgeable and experienced experts in every aspect of juvenile justice as a resource for policy makers and activists and promotes a multidisciplinary view of the issue. One of the IJJO's key objectives is to develop and support fair and effective justice reforms and strategies and to disseminate information about such programs at international conferences and other gatherings. One way the IJJO accomplishes this objective is by creating and implementing databases that act as resources for international, national, state, provincial, and local governments. The IJJO website posts interviews, articles, in-depth studies and reports, a diary of events, a statistics database, and video and audio clips of experts discussing relevant topics and ongoing IJJO efforts. The organization's newsletter can also be accessed on its website.

National Juvenile Justice Network (NJJN)
1319 F Street NW, Suite 402, Washington, DC   20004
(202) 467-0864 • fax: (202) 887-0738
website: www.njjn.org

The National Juvenile Justice Network (NJJN) is an American organization that works to support state-based groups focused on reforming the juvenile justice system. NJJN advocates for fair and equitable state and federal juvenile justice laws through education and community building. Its key objectives are to keep children out of adult correctional institutions; address racial inequalities in sentencing and incarceration; ensure access to quality legal counsel for all juveniles; improve aftercare and reentry; and obtain services for youths with special needs. NJJN publishes a number of topical reports in the field, including "Bringing Youth Home: A National Movement to Increase Public Safety, Rehabilitate Youth and Save Money" and "The Real Costs and Benefits of Change: Finding Opportunities for Reform During Difficult Financial Times." It also publishes an e-newsletter, which can be accessed on the NJJN website.

Office of Juvenile Justice and Delinquency Prevention (OJJDP)

810 Seventh Street NW, Washington, DC 20531
(202) 307-5911
website: www.ojjdp.gov

The Office of Juvenile Justice and Delinquency Prevention (OJJDP) is a component of the Office of Justice Programs in the US Department of Justice. Its job is to collaborate with professionals in the field of juvenile justice to improve existing policies and practices. The OJJDP "sponsors research, programs, and training initiatives; develops priorities and goals and sets policies to guide federal juvenile justice issues; disseminates information about juvenile justice issues; and awards funds to states to support local programming." The OJJDP publishes *OJJDP News @ a Glance*, a bimonthly e-newsletter that highlights agency activities, publications, and upcoming events, as well as the *Statistical Briefing Book*, a reliable and comprehensive collection of juvenile justice statistics.

Bibliography of Books

Robert Agnew and Timothy Brezina — *Juvenile Delinquency: Causes and Control.* 4th ed. New York: Oxford University Press, 2012.

Shahid Alvi — *Youth Criminal Justice Policy in Canada: A Critical Introduction.* New York: Springer, 2012.

Carla J. Barrett — *Courting Kids: Inside an Experimental Youth Court.* New York: New York University Press, 2012.

Maggie Blyth and Enver Solomon, eds. — *Prevention and Youth Crime: Is Early Intervention Working?* Portland, OR: Policy Press, 2009.

William J. Chambliss, ed. — *Juvenile Crime and Justice.* Thousand Oaks, CA: SAGE, 2011.

Meda Chesney-Lind and Nikki Jones, ed. — *Fighting for Girls: New Perspectives on Gender and Violence.* Albany: State University of New York Press, 2010.

Meda Chesney-Lind and Lisa Pasko, eds. — *Girls, Women, and Crime: Selected Readings.* 2nd ed. Thousand Oaks, CA: SAGE, 2013.

Chris Cunneen and Rob White — *Juvenile Justice: Youth and Crime in Australia.* 4th ed. Melbourne, Australia: Oxford University Press, 2011.

Preston Elrod and R. Scott Ryder — *Juvenile Justice: A Social, Historical, and Legal Perspective.* 3rd ed. Sudbury, MA: Jones and Bartlett Publishers, 2011.

Olivia Ferguson, ed.	*Should Juveniles Be Given Life Without Parole?* Detroit, MI: Gale Cengage Learning, 2011.
Barry Goldson, ed.	*Youth in Crisis?: 'Gangs,' Territoriality, and Violence.* New York: Routledge, 2011.
Joan Serra Hoffman, Lyndee Knox, and Robert Cohen, eds.	*Beyond Suppression: Global Perspectives on Youth Violence.* Santa Barbara, CA: Praeger, 2011.
Jeff Kunerth	*Trout: A True Story of Murder, Teens, and the Death Penalty.* Gainesville: University Press of Florida, 2012.
Friedrich Lösel, Anthony Bottoms, and David P. Farrington, eds.	*Young Adult Offenders: Lost in Transition?* New York: Routledge, 2012.
Hal Marcovitz	*Should Juveniles Be Tried as Adults?* San Diego, CA: ReferencePoint Press, 2012.
G. Larry Mays and Rick Ruddell	*Do the Crime, Do the Time: Juvenile Criminals and Adult Justice in the American Court System.* Santa Barbara, CA: Praeger, 2012.
Trevor B. Milton	*Overcoming the Magnetism of Street Life: Crime-Engaged Youth and the Programs That Transform Them.* Lanham, MD: Lexington Books, 2011.
Mairead Seymour, ed.	*Youth Justice in Context: Community, Compliance and Young People.* New York: Routledge, 2012.

Gilly Sharpe	*Offending Girls: Young Women and Youth Justice.* New York: Routledge, 2012.
Larry J. Siegel and Brandon C. Welsh	*Juvenile Delinquency: The Core.* 5th ed. Belmont, CA: Wadsworth, 2012.
Christopher Slobogin and Mark R. Fondacaro	*Juveniles at Risk: A Plea for Preventive Justice.* New York: Oxford University Press, 2011.
Roger Smith	*Doing Justice to Young People: Youth Crime and Social Justice.* New York: Willan, 2011.
J. William Spencer	*The Paradox of Youth Violence.* Boulder, CO: Lynne Rienner Publishers, 2011.
David W. Springer and Albert R. Roberts, eds.	*Juvenile Justice and Delinquency.* Sudbury, MA: Jones and Bartlett Publishers, 2011.
Mike Tapia	*Juvenile Arrest in America: Race, Social Class, and Gang Membership.* El Paso, TX: LFB Scholarly Publishers, 2012.
Jenny Vaughan	*Juvenile Crime.* Mankato, MN: Smart Apple Media, 2012.

Index

Geographic headings and page numbers in **boldface** refer to viewpoints about that country or region.

history and societal changes, 16–17

US criminalization of behavior, 59–71

See also Age of criminal responsibility

Children, Young Persons, and Their Families Act (1989, New Zealand), 75

Children Act (Ireland; 2001), 131

Children's Hearings system, Scotland, 107–108, 109–110

Children's Rights Information Network, 136

China, 180–184

crime rates, 25

current conditions of juvenile criminal justice, 183, 184

reform of juvenile justice system, 180–184

Ching, Frank, 180–184

Christchurch Health and Development Study, 77, 79–80

Citizen security, Latin America (*seguridad ciudadana*), 47–48, 49–50, 52

Clarke, Wendy, 41–42

"Class C" misdemeanors, 61, 64–65

Coarsening of culture, 34, 39–40, 57, 108, 117

Columbine High School shootings, 1999, 63

Comando Vermelho (Brazilian gang), 93, 95

Committee on the Rights of the Child (United Nations), 109, 129, 158, 199–200

Community alienation, 117

Community and social programs. *See* Social and community programs

Community policing, 94

Concept for Development of Criminal Justice for Minors (Ukraine), 206, 207

Conditional sentences, 195, 203, 204, 214–215

Condor, Sam, 117

Conduct disorder, 77–78

Confessions

capital crimes, 137, 140

coercion, 144, 145, 146, 147, 150, 151–152, 181, 187–188

Conservative Party (Canada), 171, 178

Conservative Party (United Kingdom), 163

Convention on the Rights of the Child (United Nations), 208

Argentina, 156, 157, 159, 161

Indonesia, 187

Iran, 134, 135, 139

Israel, 142, 145

Saudi Arabia, 134, 135, 139

on sentencing, 203

Sudan, 134, 135, 139

Corporal punishment, 124, 125

Costa Rica, 45, 48–50, 51

Costs of incarceration, 165, 173, 174

Council of Europe, 208–209

Crime rates

Argentina, 159, 160–161

Balkans, 31–32

Caribbean, 114–115, 117, 118

Germany, 25, 57

girls, 36

juvenile as indicator for national security, 46

Netherlands (immigrant-only), 83, 86–88

New Zealand, 76–77

rises, and tough-on-crime policies, 19, 163–164

type breakdowns, 26*t*